"Big Victory, Great Task"

"BIG VICTORY GREAT TASK"

North Viet-Nam's Minister of Defense Assesses
the Course of the War

GENERAL VO NGUYEN GIAP

INTRODUCTION BY DAVID SCHOENBRUN

FREDERICK A. PRAEGER, *Publishers*

New York • Washington • London

FREDERICK A. PRAEGER, PUBLISHERS
111 Fourth Avenue, New York, N.Y. 10003, U.S.A.
77-79 Charlotte Street, London W.1, England

Published in the United States of America in 1968
by Frederick A. Praeger, Inc., Publishers

Introduction © 1968 by Frederick A. Praeger, Inc.

Library of Congress Catalog Card Number: 67-31381

Printed in the United States of America

Introduction

The crackling static sounded like a thousand eggs frying. Everyone in the dugout tensed forward, hands cupping ears, straining to hear the messages from Dien Bien Phu. We all knew it was the end. A deep voice boomed through the static.

"This is Sergeant Millien. In five minutes everything will be blowing up here. The Viets are only a few meters away."

We heard a crash, then the voice again, "Greetings to everyone!" Another crash, a last splatter of frying eggs, then silence, the silence of death. Dien Bien Phu had fallen.

In the general staff dugout in Hanoi, the heat was choking us. Sweat poured down our faces and covered up the tears. France had suffered one of her most humiliating defeats. Ten thousand men and one woman— Geneviève de Galard, the nurse, the "Angel of Dien Bien Phu"—had been taken prisoner by the victorious troops of General Vo Nguyen Giap, who would thereafter be known as the conqueror of Dien Bien Phu.

The date was May 8, 1954, the ninth anniversary of V-E Day in Europe. It would henceforth also mark the date of the end of Western ability to influence decisively the course of history in Asia. Almost everyone knew it, except, tragically, the leaders in Washington. Eisenhower and Kennedy, in turn, tried to bolster up anti-Communists in Saigon. Then Johnson, facing the collapse

of the Saigon junta, intervened directly and made it a
new American war in Viet-Nam.

Thirteen years have now passed since Giap's troops
broke through the last trenches of the garrison at Dien
Bien Phu. Much has changed since then. America has
replaced France as the Western power trying to keep an
anti-Communist and pro-Western regime in power in
Saigon. A National Liberation Front has been created
by the revolutionaries in the South as a new force. The
NLF bears the brunt of the fighting, 200,000 southerners
fighting for their independence and for control of the
South against the Saigon military junta and 1 million
American and allied troops. The NLF is supported by
less than 50,000 men from North Viet-Nam, aiding their
"brothers" of the south. General Giap, now minister of
defense in the Hanoi government, commands, in his own
words, "the great rear area," sending aid to "the great
frontline" in the South. Dien Bien Phu is now a rural
county seat.

All these are important changes, so important that if
the situation continues to escalate, it could lead to a third
world war. But, basically, nothing has changed. The
Vietnamese revolutionaries are still fighting a war of
independence against a foreign power on their soil. The
fact that the United States is not imperialistic in the
classic French sense, in that it does not seek territory
and does not seek to colonize Viet-Nam, in no way
alters the more significant fact that it is a white, Western
nation fighting on the continent of Asia, attempting to
prevent an indigenous revolutionary movement from
coming to power in its own land. Whether that movement is Communistic or not is irrelevant to the basic fact

that American action is counterrevolutionary. This is essentially what the first Indochinese War was all about; this is essentially what the present war in Viet-Nam, the second Indochinese War, is all about. The more things change, the more they stay the same.

Ho Chi Minh, who was president of Viet-Nam in 1954, having been so recognized by the French in 1945, before they set out to reconquer their colony, is still president today. His two most faithful disciples for thirty years, Pham Van Dong and Vo Nguyen Giap, are still his right and left arms, as prime minister and defense minister respectively. Many of the "heroes of Dien Bien Phu" are still bearing arms. The legions of "people's porters," who bore the ammunition and supplies through jungles and over mountains to Dien Bien Phu on their bicycles and on their backs, are writing "a new, even more glorious chapter in the thousands-years history of resistance of the Vietnamese people," to quote their leader and the innovator of the "Legion of Porters," General Giap. It is more glorious, he proclaims, for they are now maintaining supply routes not against the relatively weak French Army but against the awesome power of destruction of the mightiest armada in the world, the U.S. air and naval forces.

In the spring of 1954, I cowered in a foxhole under the shells of Giap's artillery poured down on us from the crest of the hills over Dien Bien Phu. I wondered then how the Viets were maintaining supply lines over impassable territory under constant French fighter-bomber attack. This past summer of 1967, I again found myself cowering under shells and bombs in North Viet-Nam. This time I was behind the enemy lines, being shelled by planes of my own country, and because of that unique vantage point I was able to see with my own eyes just how the supply lines were being maintained by the same "Legion of Porters" under some of the fiercest bombing attacks of military history.

On the night of August 24, after one of the heaviest raids of the year, I rode south out of Hanoi in a Soviet-manufactured command car, with Vietnamese escort officers, along the historic Route Mandarine, now called National Route 1. It is no longer anything like a national highway. In fact, it virtually does not exist at all as a road. A few miles out of Hanoi it becomes a crater-filled obstacle course. One does not drive down it, one bounces along over ruts and rocks. Within ten miles it runs out completely, and the Route detours across a river and on to a dike. The bridge at the river crossing is out, too. There are almost no roads or bridges left intact in North Viet-Nam.

Yet the supplies keep moving, day and night, without let up, along no roads and across rivers without the benefit of bridges.

How do you move supplies without roads and bridges? By the "Legion of Porters," the brilliant logistical creation of Vo Nguyen Giap, an Asian who understands the terrain of Asia, a Vietnamese with limitless faith in the Vietnamese people, a former teacher of history with encyclopaedic knowledge of Viet-Nam's thousand-year struggle against the Chinese invaders of his country from the first century B.C. to the eighth century. Giap knows all of the tactical devices invented by his historic predecessors, from the Trung sisters and Madame Thieu, through Ly Bon, Mai Thuc Loan, Phung Hung, to the final conqueror of the Chinese, who won Vietnamese independence in 938–39, King Ngo Quyen. Giap, like all the leaders of Viet-Nam today, never fails to refer to this thousand-year struggle for independence. The very first words in this book pay tribute to this history.

The back of the coolie has been the backbone of Viet-Nam's struggle in past history. Today the backs of the people and the modern bicycle compose the supply train in the North and in the South. I saw the bicycles, with plank fixed over back wheels, weighted down at each end with straw baskets carrying up to fifty pounds each: 100 pounds per bicycle, or one ton for every twenty bicycles. And they have tens of thousands of bicycles in the "Legion of Porters." It is impossible to interdict the movement of bicycles. Bicycles do not need paved roads.

People need roads even less than bicycles do. In uncountable numbers the people of Viet-Nam, like columns of ants, lope along the rivers, across the paddies, and through the forests and jungles, with long, thin, flexible bamboo poles balanced on their shoulders, each with its straw baskets on the ends, forming the human freight trains that supply the armies and the markets of the war-ravaged land.

As for bridges, Giap has come up with a typically Vietnamese invention: the portable, floating bridge. It is astonishing to see the floating bridge put together. Flat-bottomed sampans, hidden in reeds while bombers are overhead, are floated down to the river ford, lashed together with pontoons. Then a covering of wooden planks is laid over them and traffic begins to move. I have seen ten-ton trucks with trailers cross a floating bridge.

One night, just before dawn, my car was caught in a convoy on a dike, waiting in line to cross a floating bridge. A huge truck and trailer slowly lumbered across and then lurched forward up a steep embankment on the far side. The left rear wheel sunk suddenly in a mudhole, more than hub-cap deep. I groaned at the thought of spending the entire night on the dike, in 100 degree heat under constant attack from swarms of mosquitoes more frightening than even the threat of a bombing raid on the convoy. Air raids rarely last more than five minutes and one can find cover, but mosquito raids never stop and there is no cover against Vietnamese mosquitoes.

I walked across the span bridge to watch the attempt to get the ten-ton truck out of the mudhole, an almost impossible task without a power crane. From a nearby village came a stream of peasants, each armed with a shovel and a pail or basket of sand and gravel. They covered the truck like ants on a sugar cube. Dozens of shovels dug deeply into the mud around the wheel. More dozens of sand pails and gravel scoops filled in the sucking hole, while up ahead of the truck, their backs straining against cable lines tied to the bumpers, the legion of porters pulled and hauled until inch by inch the truck moved forward and then, in one burst of liberation, exploded out of the mudhole. The entire operation took less than an hour. A crane on wheels, with a power winch, could not have done it better or more quickly. At that moment I think I fully understood for the first time what Giap and Pham Van Dong and Ho Chi Minh mean when they talk about a "people's war."

People's war is the central theme of this latest essay by Giap. He has dealt with the subject before, in greater detail, most interestingly in his guerrilla manual, *People's War, People's Army* (New York: Frederick A. Praeger, 1962). This current essay, published in book form by Praeger, is reprinted from a series of articles that appeared in September, 1967, in the Hanoi publications *Nhan Dan* and *Quan Doi Nhan Dan*. The official nature of these organs and the context of the current war, with its fierce escalation causing great material losses and human suffering, have undoubtedly conditioned the nature of the essay itself.

It is hortatory rather than expository. Giap, a heavy-handed writer to begin with, presents his argument "the Big Victory: the Great Task," as though he were haranguing a meeting of Communist cadres, which, indeed, he is. The language is cliché-ridden, larded with classic slogans, reminiscent of the very worst of Chinese Communist tracts, and infuriatingly repetitious. He argues in sweeping generalizations giving almost no specific examples to illustrate or document them. He writes, "How many troops do our people need to defeat the U.S. imperialists aggressive forces of more than 1 million men?" And he answers, "Our people in South Viet-Nam have settled this problem very satisfactorily." But he never gives the exact answer as to how many troops are needed. He does this often and also frequently belabors the obvious, such as his observation that the role of the artillery in a people's war "is to support the infantry."

One of the principal reasons for this is the fact that he is addressing himself to an audience that already knows the answers to what have become essentially rhetorical questions. Another reason, familiar to any who were in Viet-Nam at the time of the Giap articles, is the need to keep high the morale of people who are being subjected to a terrible pounding.

The American air offensive has failed in its principal objectives, as Secretary of Defense McNamara admitted in his August testimony to the Senate Sub-Committee on Preparedness. It has not significantly impeded the flow of supplies, nor has it forced Hanoi to the bargaining table. But it has succeeded in a lesser objective, making the people of North Viet-Nam pay an increasingly high cost for resistance. I suspect that it is to counter that objective that Giap has written these emotional articles, praising the resistants, boasting about the great victories of the people's forces.

Despite the clumsy style and the disappointing generalizations, these articles are interesting in themselves, as an example of the type of propaganda being used by Hanoi on the highest levels and, also, for the insight they offer into the mind of one of the key leaders, who is playing an increasingly important role as President Ho Chi Minh ages and tires and leaves more and more power in the hands of his disciples.

The fact that Ho is aging and tiring is freely admitted in Hanoi. Prime Minister Pham Van Dong told me that doctors had "advised Ho to stay away from Hanoi during the furnace heat of the summer." Except for a brief appearance on the stage the night of the anniversary of the August Revolution, Ho had not been seen in the capital for months. The effective, functioning chief, from May through September, when I left Hanoi, was the Prime Minister, not Ho. But Pham Van Dong does not have the full power and charisma of "Uncle Ho," to use the term that Ho uses himself in messages to the people, his "Dear Children." Pham Van Dong is first among equals, and, among those equals, Vo Nguyen Giap is one of the foremost.

It is important then to note, as readers of these essays will, Giap's admission that many people in South Viet-Nam were "fooled" into supporting the Saigon regime. One does not often see such an admission on so high a level. It is also most important for Americans to note how often, and with what force, Giap pays tribute to "our valorous brothers in the south." He makes it unmistakably clear that the main-line fighting, "the great frontline," is the creation of the NLF and its armed forces. He takes very little credit for his own contribution, modestly defined as the "rear" area. This is the very opposite of the Washington line that Hanoi commands all fronts and that the NLF is merely an appendage of Hanoi.

The fact that Giap says the opposite does not in itself prove he is telling the truth. But his frequent tributes to the NLF, added to Pham Van Dong's similar homage, addressed to his own people, not to the outside world, goes far toward establishing credit for the Front, credit that must add to its prestige and its own human desires to assume leadership after the war. Washington would be well advised to consider this phenomenon and its implications for future political strategy.

There is much ammunition for both hawks and doves in their controversy over the influence of China and the role of the American peace movement in the calculations of Hanoi.

Although China is virtually unmentioned, even by inference, Giap's style and his arguments are recognizably Chinese. These articles might have been translated from the Chinese rather than from the Vietnamese, to judge only by the tone and the catch phrases, particularly the frequent references to "wars of national liberation." There is almost no difference in this respect between Giap's writings and the writings of Marshal Lin Piao. Hawks will surely note this.

Doves can reply that similarities of style or even arguments do not necessarily prove subservience and that there is no evidence in the Giap articles that he is carrying out Chinese directives. The notable absence of expressions of gratitude toward China in Giap's writings and the important absence of Chinese in Viet-Nam bear witness to this. As for his use of the Lin Piao thesis on wars of national liberation, General Giap was one of the first to put these principles into practice himself in the war against France, from 1946 to 1954, somewhat before and then concurrently with Mao Tse-tung's war against Chiang. Too many people forget, and Giap's arguments can serve to remind a careful reader, that the Vietnamese war against the French broke out in the late fall of 1946, before the civil war in China, which erupted in its final, irrevocable stage, in June, 1947, after the failure of Marshall's mediation at the turn of the year.

The main tenor of his thesis is clearly, even boringly, drilled into the reader by his endless repetition of the phrase "relying mainly on our own forces." It is less a phrase than a litany. In one half-page there can be counted ten repetitions and variations of the phrase.

The title of the series, *Big Victory, Great Task*, is

most revelatory of the situation in Viet-Nam today. The key words are "Great Task." If there really were already a great victory, as Giap claims, there would not be so great a task ahead. His essays might have been more truthfully and accurately entitled "Our Great Victories and the Great Task Still Ahead."

Even Washington would not dispute the fact that the Vietnamese have won great victories by resisting for so long and so successfully the greatest power on earth. The failure of the American air offensive to interdict supplies or break the will of Hanoi must be called a victory by objective observers. It is not a final victory. Certainly the full force of American air power has not yet been unleashed. But, from early 1965 to the end of 1967, Hanoi and the NLF have, in the North and in the South, withstood more firepower than dropped on Germany in World War II and have held off more than 1 million American and allied troops with the most modern equipment.

On the other hand, Hanoi, as these Giap articles demonstrate, does not dispute the fact that there remains a great task ahead, the task of continuing to hold off possibly even greater blows. At the time this manuscript goes to press, late in October, 1967, American planes are hitting at many targets previously interdicted by the White House. In the last week of October, U.S. planes struck at the central Vietnamese Air Command Headquarters, at Phu Yen, eighteen miles northwest of Hanoi. This is the missile and MiG center, where, according to intelligence reports, there are many Russian and Chinese advisers, which is one important reason why the center was on the restricted list. At the same time, there are continuing heavy attacks seconds away from the frontiers of China. The U.S. also admitted that there were continuing overflights violating Chinese air space.

The war enters its most dangerous phase as 1967 enters into the books of history. The United States is gravely and violently divided over the issue of Viet-Nam. Many respectable people had joined the peace movement, and Giap takes note of this in his writings. But many disreputable and violent citizens also swelled the ranks of the peace movement. At the same time, the police across the country have become more violent and more brutal in its reactions to the civil disobedience of peace marchers. The leaders of Hanoi are aware of this and discussed it freely with me in late summer. As Pham Van Dong put it, "We are grateful for the help of American peace demonstrators, but, in the final analysis, we know we must count mainly on ourselves."

The Prime Minister and, even more so, President Ho are cautious about trying to exploit the divisions inside America. Giap is less cautious in his utterances, but it must at all times be remembered that Giap does not address himself to American or foreign audiences. That is the realm of the political and diplomatic leaders, not of the military. Giap did not write his articles for an American audience. He wrote for Communist and military cadres inside North Viet-Nam, and this book must be judged in that context alone.

In that context it becomes clear that his principal aim is to whip up the cadres to a new burst of patriotism and courage for the tasks ahead. Despite all his boasts of victory, Giap is a hard-headed realist. He knows the war of resistance has not yet been won. It is his job to see to it that his people do not lose heart, that they continue to believe in the final victory, and that they continue to accept the terrible sacrifices that this war is making them bear. That is surely why a major part of this text is devoted to the sacrifices of the American people and to the agonizing divisions tearing at the fabric of American society. Apparently, Giap, an experienced social psychologist, believes that one of the best ways to keep up the morale of a sorely tried people is to point out that the adversary is hurting even more.

There is a heavy dose of propaganda in these essays by Giap. The propaganda, however, is based just as heavily on reality, the reality of the resistance spirit of a valorous people, whatever else they may be.

DAVID SCHOENBRUN

Publisher's Note

We are publishing this statement by General Vo Nguyen Giap, North Vietnamese Minister of Defense, as a service to readers seriously interested in understanding the thoughts, attitudes, and aspirations of a leading Communist military tactician and political leader. This is, of course, a propaganda document, and the introduction by David Schoenbrun seeks to give it the focus of reality. General Giap's statement, including its chapter headings, is reprinted here in its entirety, as translated directly from the Vietnamese, without further comment or interpretation. The original Vietnamese version was serialized in *Nhan Dan* and *Quan Doi Nhan Dan* (Hanoi, North Viet-Nam), September 14–16, 1967.

Contents

"Big Victory, Great Task"

Our people are living the most glorious years and months in the history of our thousands-year-old fight against foreign aggression and in that of the decades-old revolutionary struggle under the leadership of our party. In the heroic south, with 170,000 square kilometers of land, they are defeating more than 1 million troops of the U.S. imperialist aggressors and their lackeys and winning bigger and bigger victories. In the north, our army and people are defeating the U.S. imperialists' war of destruction and thwarting their basic plot while pursuing socialist construction and economic development, consolidating national defense, and fulfilling the duties of the great rear toward the great frontline.

These glorious victories reflect the mountain-moving and river-filling power of our nation and people. This power is undefeatable! The anti-U.S., national salvation program of our party, which is very correct, makes our people and our armed forces invincible. The sympathy and support of brotherly socialist countries and of progressive people all over the world for our people's anti-U.S., national salvation cause have grown daily and become increasingly effective.

In the enthusiastic atmosphere, of carrying out production and fighting, commemorating the August Revolution and September 2 national day anniversaries, looking back at the anti-U.S., national salvation resistance during the past two years, and fully realizing the significance of our big victories and the heavy defeats of the enemy, our army and people are increasingly proud of and confident in our nation, our people, and beloved President Ho. Our nation and people are resolved to heighten their determination to fight, step up their great national salvation resistance, crush all the aggressive plots of the U.S. imperialists, and advance toward final victory.

I

*The Situation of the
Anti-U.S., National
Salvation Resistance During
the Past Two Years*

The Binh Gia victory in January, 1965, by the southern army and people marked the fundamental defeat of the special-war strategy of the U.S. imperialists in the south of our country. Faced with this situation, the U.S. imperialists, panic-stricken and on the defensive, resorted to all measures to save the puppet authorities and army, who were facing the danger of grave collapse. From the beginning to the middle of 1965, they carried out a makeshift strategy by hastily introducing a number of American fighting units into the south; at the same time, they expanded the war to the north by using their air force and navy continually to wage a war of destruction, thus hoping to prevent the collapse of the Saigon puppet authorities and army, consolidate and strengthen the reactionary puppet forces in the south, and save their special-war strategy from defeat. However, the situation continued to develop unfavorably for the U.S. imperialists and their lackeys.

Fired with enthusiasm by victories, our people throughout the country unanimously rose up to resist the Americans for national salvation. They continued to develop the initiative on the battlefield and attack the enemy elsewhere.

After the Binh Gia victory, between February and June, 1965, on the basis of combining armed with political struggle, the southern army and people stepped up the guerrilla war and, at the same time, developed large-scale attacks, completely beating puppet troops into a state of collapse, unable to resist the strong attacks of the Liberation Armed Forces (LAF).*

At that time, the freshly introduced U.S. troops received heavy blows at An Tan, Nui Thanh, Pleiku, Da Nang, and especially Van Tuong. They were tightly encircled in their bases by the guerrilla belts. Neither the United States nor the puppet forces were able to

---

* The official Communist designation for the Viet-Cong.—Ed.

stop the massive, continuous, and victorious attacks of the southern army and people. The U.S. imperialists and their lackeys became increasingly confused.

In the north, as of February 7, 1965, when the U.S. imperialists began using their air force to carry out attacks, our army and people dealt resounding blows to the U.S. Air Force, causing the imperialists to suffer heavy losses and become more defensive. Faced with this state of defeat and danger, and especially faced with the fact that the puppet troops were being repeatedly attacked and annihilated toward the end of 1965, U.S. President Johnson, after forcing General Taylor to resign, decided to introduce massive U.S. expeditionary troops into South Viet-Nam to participate directly in combat, thus shifting the aggressive war to a new strategic phase: the limited-war strategy.

In October, 1965, after introducing 180,000 U.S. expeditionary troops into South Viet-Nam, thus increasing the total of American and puppet troops to 700,000 men, the U.S. imperialists launched their first strategic counter-offensive with the extravagant hope of quickly destroying the regular units of the southern liberation forces and ending the war in 1966. This strategic counteroffensive was developed in the form of two successive major operations during the 1965–66 dry season.

The first operation was launched during the winter of 1965 with a large force, composed of many of the most seasoned units of the U.S. armed forces, such as the 1st Airmobile Division, the 1st Infantry Division, paratroop units, and so forth. The U.S. imperialists launched their attacks in two main directions: north of Saigon and the high plateaus, where they believed the liberation troops were concentrating their main forces. Contrary to the desires of the U.S. imperialists, both these attacks failed.

After their heavy defeat in Van Tuong, the Americans and puppets lost many battalions in Bau Bang, Dau Tieng, north of Saigon, Plei Me, the high plateaus, and other areas. Thus, the U.S. troops were defeated right at the beginning. McNamara was very surprised, and Washington was flabbergasted. They hastily increased the number of American fighting men, and then launched their second tide of attacks in the spring of 1966.

At the time, the total of U.S. troops reached 250,000 men. They poured their entire mobile force into a five-pronged attack, which was aimed in three main directions: eastern Nam Bo, the Trung Bo Delta, and the high plateaus, with the aim of annihilating the LAF and, simultaneously, carrying out pacification. But again, they failed ignominiously. During this wave of large-scale attacks, the enemy used as many as twenty-seven battalions in some battles, such as at Bong Son and Binh Dinh. But it was unable to annihilate any liberation detachment. On the contrary, U.S. and puppet troops suffered heavy losses in Cu Chi, Nha Do, Bong Trang, eastern Nam Bo, Phu Yen, Quang Ngai, Binh Dinh, the Trung Bo Delta, the high plateaus, and so on. The first dry-season strategic counteroffensive of the U.S. imperialists ended tragically, with more than thirty battalions annihilated, of which fourteen were U.S. and satellite infantry battalions, and more than 110,000 troops killed or wounded, of whom more than 40,000 were U.S. and satellite troops.

In the 1965–66 winter-spring period, while U.S. troops sustained heavy defeats during the initial fighting and the puppet troops were continuously on the defensive, the southern army and people, on the contrary, maintained and developed their initiative on the battlefields and stepped up guerrilla and large-scale attacks. They took the initiative in counterattacking and destroying the enemy in his various operations and, at the same time, in attacking and annihilating the enemy deep in his rear—such as the attacks against his lair in Saigon, his barracks and logistic bases in various areas, and so forth.

The southern army and people defeated American puppet and satellite troops right in the first round of the limited war of the U.S. imperialists. On the basis of the 1965–66 winter-spring victories, the southern army and people stepped up the combination of military struggle with political struggle and actively attacked the enemy, causing an unstable situation in which the puppet authorities and army encountered crises in all fields, and driving the U.S. imperialists into an embarrassed and defensive position. Thirty cities and municipalities throughout the south seethed with the struggle of city people rising up against the introduction of U.S. aggressive troops and against the Thieu-Ky clique. In Da Nang and Hue, the political movement developed most widely and vigorously during this period.

It was obvious that conflicts between the U.S. imperialists and the traitors and the southern people were becoming very fierce. The vehement attacks of the southern army and people caused the Americans and puppets to sustain heavy military defeats and encounter grave political crises. This situation brought about quarrels, conflicts, and discord among the puppet authorities and army in the I Corps area. This crisis lasted over two months and led five times to a change in commanders. Six enemy battalions were dispersed as a result of their shooting at each other.

Faced with this situation, and especially with U.S. troop defeats, the decline of the puppet troops was accelerated. In some months, there were 20,000 deserters. At the same time, many military revolts broke out, such as in the 1st Regiment at Thu Dau Mot and other puppet units.

During the summer of 1966, after the defeat of their first dry-season strategic counteroffensive, the U.S. imperialists planned to return to the defensive, avoid the major attacks of the liberation troops, and actively reinforce and increase American expeditionary troops in order to prepare for their new strategic counteroffensive during the 1966–67 dry season. But during the summer of 1966, American and puppet troops continued to suffer repeated attacks from the southern army and people on all important strategic battlefields from Tri Thien, the high plateaus, and central Trung Bo to eastern, central, and western Nam Bo.

During the 1966–67 dry season, after having reinforced and increased U.S. expeditionary troops to 400,-000 men, thus boosting the total of American and puppet troops to over 1 million men, the U.S. imperialists launched their second strategic counteroffensive. The projected main characteristics of this major counteroffensive were: (1) carrying out a two-pronged strategic plan—search-and-destroy and pacification raids; (2) using the experience of defeat in their first counteroffensive so that this time they could concentrate on carrying out the main tasks of the new counteroffensive; (3) achieving a new distribution of labor between the two strategic forces, with the U.S. forces being in charge of the search-and-destroy mission while the puppet regulars were responsible for pacification.

With a very large military force, the U.S. imperialists launched their counteroffensive, this time with the aim of destroying the areas in which, they believed, resistance organs were concentrated, trying to annihilate the liberation regulars; they stepped up the pacification task in order to change the situation, to win a victory of strategic significance in a short period, and to solve the Vietnamese problem quickly. But the U.S. imperialists again encountered heavy defeats during this second dry-season strategic counteroffensive and faced a more serious defensive state.

In early winter of 1966, carrying out the South Vietnamese National Liberation Front (NLF) Central Committee's appeal, of October 17, 1966, resolutely to fight and defeat the U.S. aggressors during the 1966–67 winter-spring period, the southern army and people prepared to counterattack the enemy and, simultaneously initiated new attacks on all battlefields. After the summer of 1966 ended, the southern army and people opened a new battlefield in Tri Thien, attacking the U.S. and puppet troops strongly and repeatedly, and forcing them to bring U.S. troops from other fields and disperse them to cope with various attacks on this battlefield.

This was a big surprise for the U.S. imperialists, which caused them to become passive and embarrassed before pouring their forces into their second dry-season strategic counteroffensive. In the high plateau area, the LAF lured the U.S. troops into coming to Plei Djereng and annihilated them in bloody battles along the banks of the Sa Thay River. On the Nam Bo battlefield, especially in the Nam Bo Delta, the southern army and people developed a new offensive situation.

The southern LAF inaugurated the 1966–67 winter-spring victories by attacking the Long Binh bomb depot on October 28 and shelling the military parade of the U.S.–puppet clique in the heart of Saigon on November 1. These were heavy blows to the enemy.

In eastern Nam Bo, the main target of U.S. troop attacks throughout the 1966–67 winter-spring period, the enemy launched many military operations. The most important were Attleboro, Cedar Falls, and Junction City. These were defensive operations, aimed at coping with the fierce attacks of the Nam Bo troops and people. For the Attleboro campaign, the enemy mobilized over 30,000 troops. But the campaign ended with heavy losses for the 196th Brigade, units of the 25th Division, the Tropic Lightening, the 1st Division, the Big Red One, the 173d Brigade, and so forth.

The Junction City campaign, begun in February, 1967, was one into which the Americans poured the largest number of troops in order to take a single objective during this dry season. They poured a large force—composed of 45,000 troops and a large number of planes, artillery pieces, and armored vehicles—into a battlefield of less than 400 square kilometers with the hope of achieving a decisive victory. But this largest campaign was dealt the greatest defeat, which ignominiously ended the second dry-season strategic counter-offensive of the Americans.

The search-and-destroy operations of the Americans and puppets had failed. Naturally, their pacification task achieved no results.

While fighting fiercely, the southern army and people continued to step up the coordination of the military and political struggles. The political struggle movement of the southern city people continued to develop strongly. Its anti-U.S. character increased. The southern people's liberated areas continued to be firmly maintained, and some liberated areas were even enlarged. The bitter failure of the U.S. pacification plan was marked by the dismissal of Cabot Lodge and Lansdale. Thus, in the second strategic counteroffensive, the U.S. imperialists were defeated more heavily than in the first. Some 175,000 troops were annihilated, including more than 70,000 U.S. troops. A total of ninety-nine battalions and battalion-size units, including twenty-eight U.S. battalions, were put out of action. Some 3,000 aircraft, hundreds of artillery pieces, and other equipment were destroyed.

The U.S. imperialists and their lackeys have been increasingly bogged down and constantly passive. They could not destroy even one small unit of the liberation troops' main force, and were annihilated in great numbers. They could not gain the initiative, but had passively to resist our forces on all battlefields.

They have suffered the heaviest defeats wherever the greatest bulk of their forces was concentrated. They planned to send troops to the Mekong River Delta, but had to postpone this because the situation on all battlefields was very difficult for them and their lackeys. They intended to save the puppet troops, but the regular puppet troops continued to decline and lose their fighting ability, even in the pacification task.

This summer, following the failure of the second dry-season strategic counteroffensive, a pessimistic atmosphere has enveloped the U.S. ruling clique and the Vietnamese traitors in Saigon. The U.S. aggressors and their lackeys were greatly disturbed by the increasingly serious and insurmountable political and military difficulties and deadlock. They are embarrassed by the increasingly stronger offensive of the southern army and people and the determination of all the Vietnamese people to oppose the Americans for national salvation. They are encountering the increasingly firm opposition of progressive people in the world and even in the United States.

The ruling clique in the White House and the Pentagon have fiercely quarreled with one another about the seriously stalemated U.S. situation in Viet-Nam. Westmoreland was called back to the United States to deliver a speech in which he deceitfully said that there was no stalemate, but he himself had to ask Johnson to send many more reinforcements to the south. U.S. Defense Secretary McNamara, who hurriedly went to Saigon for the ninth time in order to study all aspects of the war, openly criticized Westmoreland for wasting human strength and told him to increase the efficiency of U.S. troops now on hand in Viet-Nam.

Following this, Taylor, a U.S. strategist, and Clifford, a U.S. intelligence ringleader, toured the satellite countries of the United States in Southeast Asia in order to recruit more mercenary troops, but failed to attain the results desired by the U.S. imperialists.

It is clear that the American imperialists have been increasingly stalemated, following the second strategic counteroffensive. Their limited war has been disastrously defeated. As for the southern army and people, following the 1966–67 winter-spring feats of arms, a stimulating, confident, and seething atmosphere has been reigning over all battlefields and has urged the southern army and people to move forward to score greater and more resounding achievements.

The LAF has matured swiftly and gained much more fighting experience and has shown that it is in very good shape. This summer, with the impetus of big victories, the southern army and people continue to develop their initiative, intensify both military and political offensives everywhere, and deal the U.S. puppet and satellite troops painful blows in Con Tien, Gioc Mieu, Gio An, Nong Son, Mo Duc, Tan Uyen, Can Le, My Tho, and Quoi Son, and at many airbases, such as Da Nang, Chu Lai, and elsewhere. The above was the war situation in the south during the past two years.

In the same period, in the northern part of our country, the U.S. imperialists used an important part of the U.S. Air Force based in the 7th Fleet, in the south, and in Thailand to attack the north in an attempt to extricate themselves from their predicament in the south, shake the morale of our people in both zones, and check the northern people's support of their southern compatriots' liberation struggle. This is an important measure of the limited-war strategy and, at the same time, a desperate act of the U.S. imperialists.

At the outset, they attacked the southern areas of the Fourth Military Zone. Following this, they have gradually escalated the war against the northern part of North Viet-Nam. On several occasions, they temporarily stopped attacking the north for some time in order to deceive people with their peace tricks and to reorganize their forces, and then continued to widely escalate the war beyond the parallel.

On June 21, 22, and 28, 1966, they began rashly attacking the capital of Hanoi, thus increasing their war of destruction against the north to the most serious degree. They have also used the naval forces of the 7th Fleet and artillery units stationed south of the temporary military demarcation line to supplement the activities of their air force against the coastal areas of the military zone and the southern part of Vinh Linh. Their targets have been axes of communications, industrial sites, dams and dikes, cities, populated areas, schools, hospitals, markets, and so forth.

However, for more than two years the U.S. imperialists' war of destruction in the north has been defeated. The imperialists have been confronted with an anti-U.S., national salvation high tide of the northern army and people. To date, nearly 2,300 fighter aircraft of the U.S. imperialists have been shot down, and thousands of American pilots have been killed or captured in the north. The prestige of the U.S. Air Force has collapsed disastrously. These figures were computed as of September 14, 1967.

In the war, the north has increased the strength of the socialist regime and has fought well, along with achieving good production. The north has constantly ensured good communications and transportation and has unceasingly developed its economy and culture.

Despite many difficulties created by the enemy, the people's living conditions continue to be stabilized. The determination of our people to oppose the Americans for national salvation has been increasingly strengthened.

Meanwhile, in the south, with the spirit "The north calls, the south answers," the southern army and people have continually attacked the U.S., puppet, and satellite troops everywhere and have striven to attack their airbases and logistical depots, thus causing them to suffer heavy losses and to become increasingly defensive.

Generally speaking, the war developments during the past two years can be summarized as follows:

On the Enemy Side

1. Because of the failure of their special-war strategy, the U.S. imperialists have defensively shifted to the limited-war strategy. They have waged an unprecedentedly large limited war of aggression. With regard to military strength, they have mobilized more than 1 million troops, including 500,000 U.S. troops. As for military means, they have used about one-third of the U.S. Strategic Air Force, as many as 4,000 aircraft of all types, including some 1,300 modern fighter aircraft, and thirteen of the seventeen attack aircraft carriers of the U.S. naval force. They have used very great quantities of the most modern weapons and equipment, except for atomic weapons, in the war.

With regard to their war budget, according to their official sources, in 1966 alone the U.S. imperialists spent as much as $13 billion; they plan to increase this to $30 billion in 1967 and 1968.

The U.S. imperialists mobilized the American, puppet, and satellite forces to launch two strategic offensives in South Viet-Nam, and have continuously used their air and naval forces to attack the north. Yet they have not been able to extricate themselves from their predicament in South Viet-Nam, which is getting worse and worse.

2. The U.S. imperialists have been utterly defeated in all fields—military, political, and tactical—throughout the very important period of the limited war. All of their strategic objectives have failed. The U.S. and puppet forces have suffered heavy setbacks, while their pacification plans have gone bankrupt. The puppet administration and armed forces have weakened with every passing day. They are faced with a very bad and seriously stalemated war situation.

3. As a result of their waging the war of aggression in Viet-Nam, the U.S. imperialists are increasingly isolated in the world. The progressive people throughout the world, including the American people, have vehemently condemned the U.S. imperialists for their aggression against Viet-Nam and have risen up to struggle against them by all means. Many of the U.S. imperialists' satellite countries have shown themselves indifferent to the war of aggression in Viet-Nam. Some have even officially protested against it. Even the American ruling authorities themselves have fallen into discord and dissension in the face of their heavy setbacks in Viet-Nam.

On Our Side

1. A glance at all aspects of the anti-U.S., national salvation resistance war of our people shows that the

situation has never been as favorable as it is now. The armed forces and people in the entire country have stood up to fight the enemy and are achieving one great victory after another. In South Viet-Nam, faced with the U.S. imperialists' change of strategy, the southern armed forces and people have continued developing their initiative, have continuously attacked the enemy on all battlefields, and have defeated two large-scale strategic counteroffensives of the U.S., puppet, and satellite forces. The military struggle has been stepped up in close co-ordination with the political one, which is becoming increasingly deep and wide. The resistance forces of the southern combatants and people are growing rapidly in number and strength.

In North Viet-Nam, our armed forces and people have defeated and are defeating the U.S. imperialists' war of destruction, have continued building socialism, and at the same time have striven to fulfill the duty of a large rear toward a large frontline. North Viet-Nam is growing increasingly strong and steady in all fields.

2. The victories achieved by the armed forces and people in the entire country have been of great political and strategic significance. Our people throughout the country are standing shoulder to shoulder in steadily advancing and pushing the anti-U.S., national salvation resistance war to final victory.

3. Our people's anti-U.S., national salvation resistance war is just, and it is aimed at safeguarding the people's independence and freedom. It is also of great international significance; consequently, it is strongly approved of and supported by brother socialist countries and progressive people all over the world. Never has our people's re-

sistance war against foreign aggression been so strongly encouraged and supported by the world's peoples as it is now. The world's revolutionary people consider the anti-U.S., national salvation resistance war of our people as an anti-U.S. frontline of the world's peoples and a center of the present national liberation struggle movement.

The U.S. Imperialists Were
Heavily Defeated During
the Very Important Period
of the Strategy of
Limited War in South
Viet-Nam

Ever since World War II, and especially after their defeats in China, Korea, Indochina, and Cuba, the U.S. imperialists have sensed the inferiority of the imperialist camp and their own in the world balance of power. The imperialist camp, led by the American imperialists, has been forced to take a passive and defensive position in the face of the growth of the socialist camp, of the seething and mounting national liberation movement, and of the continuous offensive posture of the revolutionary movement in the world.

The U.S. imperialists have had to give up their massive retaliation strategy and adopt that of the flexible response. They maintain that the flexible-response strategy, which includes three forms of war—special war, limited war, and total war—is the most suitable of those that may help them find a way out of their passiveness when they are not in a position to prosecute a nuclear war. They add that it is the most positive strategy for implementing their aggressive policy and performing their function as an international gendarme in coping with the national liberation movement, which is rising like a storm throughout the world, and to prepare for aggression against socialist countries. They call the special war and the local war a sharp sword that cuts into the national liberation movement, creating favorable conditions for them to prepare for a world war.

In the south of our country, the U.S. imperialists resorted to the special war and failed. They had to shift hastily and defensively to the limited-war strategy to cope with their dangerous situation. This act not only reflected their failure, but also laid bare their obdurate, aggressive, and warlike nature.

What is the U.S. imperialists' limited-war strategy? According to their views, limited war is one of the three forms of their aggressive war. It is an actual war for the Americans, but with limitations as far as size and scope are concerned. Differing from special war, mainly waged by local lackey troops, U.S. imperialist limited war is waged directly by U.S. troops.

But the general aggressive policy of the American imperialists is aimed at achieving neocolonialism. Thus, when they wage limited war in order to repress the national liberation movement, they must brazenly use local troops and puppet authorities to wage war along with U.S. troops. They regard the puppet troops and authorities as an important buttress.

In the U.S. imperialists' limited wars, aimed at achieving their aggressive neocolonialist policy, the final goal that the war must achieve is the consolidation of the puppet army and government and their transformation into effective tools for the achievement of neocolonialism. The main military goal of the limited-war strategy is annihilating the enemy's military forces. The philosophy of this strategy is to attack and attack quickly in order to solve the war quickly.

The prominent characteristic of the limited-war strategy is to use U.S. troops in direct aggression while limiting the war scope; to win military victory in the shortest possible time; and to create conditions for realizing the enslaving domination of neocolonialism.

Limiting the number of U.S. troops means using only a certain part of the military forces of the U.S. infantry, air force, and navy in the limited war. The American imperialists must restrict the U.S. forces participating in a limited war, because without this restriction, their global strategy will encounter difficulties and their influence over the world will be affected. They must achieve this limitation to avoid upsetting political, economic, and social life in the United States. This means that although they wage the war, they do not have to mobilize their forces and they continue to carry out their economic and social programs in the United States.

They impose this restriction because they are convinced that they can achieve victory even if they use only a limited number of troops to participate directly in a local war aimed at repressing the national liberation movement in any given country in Asia, Africa, or Latin America.

Having to restrict the number of U.S. troops, the American imperialists pay special attention to consolidating and using the forces of local lackeys. They believe that if they use a limited number of U.S. troops as a core for local lackey troops, equipped with modern weapons, to wage a local aggressive war in the countries where the economy is relatively backward or newly developed, they will be able to repress their adversaries, thanks to their superiority in military force and firepower, and will be victorious in a short time. Restricting the strategic goals means restricting the political goals of the war and, in the military field, concentrating forces in order quickly to destroy the adversary's military forces—especially its regulars. They must do this so that they can avoid having to disperse their troops to different targets and so that they can fight and resolve the war quickly.

They believe that the adversary's backbone is its armed forces, and that if they can defeat these, they can end the war, but that if they cannot do so, the war will last a long time, and they will be defeated. They must win, because they want to create favorable conditions for the lackey forces to fulfill the tasks following victory, thus allowing the imperialists to bring their troops home quickly but still to maintain political conditions to achieve neocolonialism.

Restricting the scope of the war means waging war only in a certain country or area, thus preventing it from ravaging other nations or regions. They believe that if they cannot limit the scope of the war, they will become more defensive and face greater defeats, because bigger countries will be forced to join in. As of now they have not finished making preparations for a new world war.

The U.S. imperialists can restrict the limited war to a certain country or area, depending upon concrete conditions. But no matter what the scope is, their objective continues to be quickly to annihilate the revolutionary forces and pursue the achievement of neocolonialism.

Having in mind the above-mentioned views about the limited-war strategy of the U.S. imperialists, we note that the limited war that the American imperialists are waging in South Viet-Nam has exceeded the original restrictions as far as scope is concerned. American forces have far exceeded the confinements of limited wars, for each of which they may mobilize only between three and six divisions. U.S. and satellite forces now in South Viet-Nam equal eleven divisions (of which nine are American and two are South Korean).

The U.S. troops' strategic objectives on the southern battlefield are not restricted to annihilating the LAF, but have included the task of pacification. To begin with, as far as the scope of the war is concerned, the U.S. imperialists have exceeded the restriction of limiting the war to South Viet-Nam. They have been using their air force and navy to wage a war of destruction against

North Viet-Nam; they are continuing to intervene more and more strongly in the Laotian kingdom and brazenly provoke the Cambodian kingdom; and they are planning to expand the war to the entire Indochinese peninsula in order to extricate themselves from their dangerous situation in South Viet-Nam.

In the south of our country, when the U.S. imperialists shifted to the limited-war strategy, they obviously pursued the achievement of neocolonialism. Therefore, although they have sent hundreds of thousands of American troops to the south, they still have had to strive to consolidate the puppet army and administration as a necessary political and military support for their neocolonialist war of aggression. They still capitalize on the name of the puppet administration and strive to consolidate its army.

Along with the military tricks of the war of aggression, they have feverishly carried out the political tricks of neocolonialism. Consequently, the U.S. imperialists' present limited war still is an aggressive war aimed at achieving the political objectives of neocolonialism; it is a neocolonialist war of aggression. The limited-war strategy in particular and that of flexible reaction in general are products of the U.S. imperialists' bourgeois military thinking which have come into existence in circumstances under which imperialism has become increasingly depressed, defeated, and defensive in the face of a situation in which the balance of power in the world is not favorable for them.

Like their neocolonialist policy of aggression, the U.S. imperialists' limited-war strategy is full of contradictions and insurmountable basic weaknesses. In essence, these are the inherent contradictions and weaknesses of an unjust war of aggression. In the southern part of our country, these contradictions and weaknesses have increasingly worsened and have clearly revealed themselves in the process of development of the U.S. imperialists' war of aggression and of our people's anti-U.S., national salvation resistance.

Since they started the limited war and began to send U.S. troops to wage direct aggression against the south and to use their air force and navy to stage raids against the north, the U.S. imperialists have brazenly revealed their cruel aggressive face and have made the contradictions between themselves and their lackeys and all the Vietnamese people increasingly acute on a national scale. The contradictions between the Vietnamese people and the American imperialists and their lackeys are the main contradictions which will determine the failure of the U.S. imperialists' war of aggression.

The U.S. imperialists have encountered the resistance of an active people, who are courageous, undaunted, full of fighting experiences, and united as one. The south and the north have unanimously taken up arms and have fought shoulder to shoulder for the just cause and for the complete independence and freedom of the fatherland.

In sending U.S. troops to South Viet-Nam, the U.S. imperialists have encountered a people's war which has developed to a high degree and is in an offensive position. This people's war has successfully developed the people's strength, has succeeded in mobilizing all the people to fight the aggressors militarily and politically in all ways and with all kinds of weapons—from primitive to modern—and has created a very great combined strength.

This great people's war has gloriously defeated the U.S. imperialists' special war and is on an irreversible course of vigorous development. Events have proved that from the time they began to send U.S. troops to wage direct aggression in the south, the U.S. imperialists have been defeated. They are being compelled to scatter their forces and are in a defensive position on all battlefields. In waging the war of aggression against the north, the U.S. imperialists have knocked their heads against a firm steel bastion.

To protect the north, liberate the south, and proceed toward reunifying the country, the northern armed forces and people have stepped up and are stepping up the violent people's fight against the U.S. aggressors' war of destruction. The northern armed forces and people have developed their revolutionary heroism to a high degree, have defeated the U.S. imperialists' war of destruction, and have fulfilled wholeheartedly and to the best of their ability the obligation of the large rear base toward the large frontline.

By sending U.S. troops to wage direct aggression in South Viet-Nam, and by using their air force to stage raids against the north, which is an independent and sovereign country and a component of the socialist camp, the U.S. imperialists have made more acute their conflicts with the socialist camp, the national liberation movement, and the progressive people of the world. The more the U.S. imperialists intensify their war of aggression in Viet-Nam, the more resolutely they make the socialist countries oppose them and cause them more positively to help the Vietnamese people in order to protect a member country of the socialist camp and an outpost of socialism, and to fulfill the socialist nations' glorious obligation toward the national liberation movement.

The progressive people of the world have supported more and more vigorously the Vietnamese people's struggle against the U.S. aggressors and are attacking them everywhere in the world. The U.S. imperialists are meeting with vigorous protests from the progressive people of the world, including the American people.

The U.S. imperialists have pursued a policy of neocolonialist aggression. Yet they have had to send U.S. troops to wage direct aggression in South Viet-Nam. This has heightened the contradictions between their aim of imposing neocolonialism and their trick of using U.S. troops to prosecute the war. By sending U.S. troops to wage direct aggression in the south, the U.S. imperialists have clearly revealed their brazen aggressive face, which they cannot cover. These contradictions have deepened many basic political problems of neocolonialism and led the U.S. imperialists toward many difficulties and defeats.

The U.S. imperialists' introduction of troops into the south has been aimed at preventing the collapse of the puppet army and administration and creating new conditions for consolidating and strengthening the puppet forces.

Yet, the more the war of aggression is Americanized, the more disintegrated the puppet Saigon army and administration becomes. The traitorous and country-selling nature of the leaders of the puppet army and administration has been exposed. They have been cursed by all our people.

Furthermore, the internal contradictions of the puppet army and administration and the conflicts between the U.S. imperialists and the puppet army and administration have increasingly developed. Those in the puppet army and administration who still have some national spirit have become gradually enlightened. More and more of them have returned to the people. Faced with the towering crimes of the U.S. aggressors and the country-selling traitors, the southern people have become more full of hatred, have reinforced their solidarity, and have fought valiantly and resolutely for final victory under the National Liberation Front's anti-U.S., national salvation banner.

The more they increase the number of their troops in the south and the more they extend the fighting, the more the U.S. imperialists deepen the contradictions between their limited-war strategy and their global strategy. The more the limited war in the south is stepped up, the more adversely it will affect the other positions of the U.S. imperialists around the world—especially when they have had to mobilize forces for a limited war which has far exceeded their estimates. As a result, the contradictions between their limited-war strategy and their global strategy have become more acute.

The world revolutionary people can take advantage of this situation to intensify their attacks against the U.S. imperialists, with a view to repulsing them step by step and eliminating them piece by piece. The U.S. imperialists' allies can also take advantage of this situation to bargain for their own interests, thus creating difficulties for the American imperialists.

In the southern part of our country, during the past two years the U.S. imperialists' limited-war strategy has revealed many basic weaknesses. First of all, the American imperialists' limited-war strategy was adopted on the base of the defeat of the special-war strategy—the U.S. imperialists have sent troops to the south into a defensive and defeated position and in a situation in which the puppet army and administration have been on the decline. As a result, from the outset, their limited-war strategy has become a defensive strategy, and a very unfavorable strategic position was forced upon them.

By waging a limited war, the U.S. imperialists have hoped to ward off the decline of the puppet army and administration, so that they could use them to support politically and militarily their neocolonialist war of aggression. Yet, in the southern part of our country, the puppet army and administration have become impotent and increasingly weakened.

The introduction of American expeditionary troops into the south has been aimed at providing military support for the puppet army. Yet U.S. troops have sustained continuous defeats and serious losses. The U.S. and puppet troops have not been able to rely upon each other, support each other, or coordinate with each other. As a result, their strategic effect has been reduced. The U.S. imperialists have developed their limited-war strategy in an extremely defensive situation. The puppet army and administration have become impotent.

However, the American imperialists have encountered the Vietnamese people who have a determination to fight and win a great people's war, and who have developed to a high degree creative strategy and tactics, and an invincible strength. Therefore, the serious defeats sustained by American troops have been inevitable.

In the unjust war of aggression in the south, the U.S. expeditionary forces have been fighting without an ideal and, as a result, their morale has been very low. The more they are defeated, the worse this basic weakness becomes. Furthermore, although they are numerous and equipped with modern armaments, they have encountered very great difficulties: topography, climate, and organization, and training which is not suitable to the Vietnamese battlefield. Unaccustomed to the topography and climate, American troops have encountered very great difficulties.

How has the U.S. imperialists' strategic defeat developed during the past two years, during which they have waged a limited war in South Viet-Nam? As we all know, when they introduced troops into the south, the U.S. imperialists wanted to use their great military superiority, concentrate their forces, and launch an offensive in an attempt to annihilate the LAF and regain the initiative. Yet, although they have more than 1 million troops at their disposal, they so far have not been able to realize this strategic design. Although they wanted to concentrate their forces, they have had to scatter them in many theaters and assign them many tasks. From the time they were introduced into the south until the end of 1966, the U.S. expeditionary troops were compelled to scatter in three major theaters—eastern Nam Bo, the highlands, and central Trung Bo—to cope with the vigorously developing people's war.

Recently, U.S. troops have been scattered in another area: the Quang Tri-Thua Thien theater. Generally speaking, on the southern battlefield, American forces have been scattered almost equally in these four theaters.

This dispersed deployment of strategic forces runs counter to the American military leaders' plans. It is bitter for the U.S. imperialists to realize that in each of these four theaters, U.S. troops have been thinly scattered.

In the First Army Corps area, U.S. Marines have been dispersed over an area of approximately 500 to 600 kilometers. In the highlands, U.S. forces, which are not large, have been scattered over a 200-kilometer area. In eastern Nam Bo, American troops have had to spread out on many fronts and have found it necessary to defend all areas. As a result, large U.S. forces have become small and have failed to yield adequate strength.

U.S. and puppet troops have not only been scattered in many theaters but have been also assigned many tasks. It has been the U.S. imperialists' intention to concentrate their and puppet forces on wiping out the LAF and, thereby, rapidly settling the war. Yet, faced with the southern people's mounting military and political struggle from the rural areas to the cities, the imperialists have had to assign U.S. and puppet troops to pacification. The assignment of the bulk of the regular units of the puppet army to pacification is a strategic setback. The assignment of U.S. and satellite troops to pacification will certainly lead the U.S. imperialists to great political and military reversals.

Although the American imperialists wanted to launch an offensive, they have fallen into a defensive position.

It is an extremely dangerous thing for any aggressive army to have forces scattered, and to remain on the defensive is even more dangerous.

At present, about 70 per cent of the U.S. troops perform defensive tasks in South Viet-Nam. According to the Pentagon's calculations, at least 200,000 troops are needed to defend U.S. bases of various sizes in South Viet-Nam. To defend the Da Nang airbase alone, the U.S. imperialists have mobilized one division of American troops and deployed them over a 25-kilometer perimeter. Recently, the U.S. imperialists estimated that only one out of eight U.S. servicemen in South Viet-Nam is engaged in mobile combat. McNamara admitted that the combat efficiency of U.S. troops is very low. He found that of the nearly 500,000 American troops in South Viet-Nam, only 70,000 are directly engaged in combat.

The U.S. imperialists have had to commit their combat forces to the defense of their bases, cities, military lines of communications, and even the puppet army, which is being shaken, depressed, and disintegrated. As a result, although U.S. troops are very numerous, they are thinly spread and lack offensive strength.

The U.S. imperialists wanted to destroy the LAF, but they have been seriously annihilated. During the past two years on the southern battlefield, they have feverishly concentrated efforts on trying to extricate themselves from their scattered and defensive position. They have continuously increased the number of their troops and have conducted offensive operations. Yet they have failed. They sustained very serious defeats in the two "dry-season strategic counteroffensives."

Why do the U.S. and puppet troops not have strategic

effect and combat efficiency, although they have conducted many battalion-sized, division-sized, and even multidivision-sized search-and-destroy operations?

To wipe out the enemy it is necessary, first of all, to concentrate forces. The American troops have been scattered to cope with the comprehensive and powerful people's war. They have not only failed to concentrate their offensive forces, but have also been compelled to fight according to the will of the southern LAF. In actual combat, in most of the battles, American troops have failed to find their targets, not because the U.S. imperialists lack modern reconnaissance instruments, but because in the people's war in South Viet-Nam, which has developed to a high degree, targets and battlefronts exist everywhere, yet do not exist anywhere.

The prevalent phenomenon emerging from the war in South Viet-Nam is that U.S. troops have always been surprised, caught in the LAF's traps, and destroyed. They have not been able to wipe out the LAF; on the contrary, they have been seriously annihilated, although they are very numerous and have continuously conducted search-and-destroy operations. This is a strategic and tactical defeat sustained by American troops on the southern battlefield.

The U.S. imperialists wanted to regain the initiative. Yet they have fallen deeper and deeper into a defensive position. As everyone knows, initiative on the battlefield is manifested by the fact that one can act freely and at will, that one is fully free to choose the place and time for launching attacks, and that one can maneuver the enemy and compel him to adopt the fighting methods one selects. The most important factor is that one must succeed in destroying the enemy.

On the southern battlefield during the past two years, American troops have not had freedom of action, have been compelled to fight on the terms of the southern armed forces and people, and have not been able to annihilate any section of the LAF. How can they regain the initiative on the battlefields?

During the past two years, American forces have been very eager to destroy the LAF in eastern Nam Bo, in the highlands, in the delta of the Fifth Zone, and in the Tri Thien region. Yet it is in these areas that the U.S. expeditionary troops have sustained serious destructive blows. The Americans have not yet been able to carry out their plan to introduce their troops into the Mekong Delta.

During the past two years, U.S. troops have exerted extensive efforts and conducted thousands of operations of various sizes. Yet they have failed to regain the initiative.

It may seem that American forces have taken the initiative in conducting these operations, which appear to have an offensive character. Yet, in essence they have had neither combat efficiency nor strategic effect. Therefore, U.S. troops have fallen deeper and deeper into a defensive position.

Though wanting to engage in a *blitzkrieg*, the U.S. imperialists have been forced to fight a protracted war. The leading strategic idea of the imperialists' aggressive war is to fight quickly in order to end the war quickly. Waging limited aggressive war in South Viet-Nam under the present situation in the world and the United States, the U.S. imperialists want to fight quickly. But they have been forced to fight a protracted war, although they have boosted the aggressive war to a large scale. They have encountered an adversary—the southern army and people—who is both resolute and clever and who has successfully thwarted their *blitzkrieg* plots since the day they started implementing their special-war strategy. They could not fight quickly because they did not know their adversary and because they overestimated their own strongpoints of numerical strength and modern weapons.

The fact that the American imperialists have been forced to fight a protracted war is a big defeat for them. The more protracted the war is, the more fierce will be the basic contradictions and weaknesses of the aggressive war of the U.S. imperialists in South Viet-Nam—contradictions and weaknesses that will lead them to increasingly big defeats.

The imperialists have been unable to pacify the countryside and stabilize the situation in the cities. They have used the majority of the puppet troops and a part of their own forces to fulfill the pacification task, but they have failed ignominiously. The pacification plan has not made any progress, and the situation in the cities has become increasingly more troubled. They have bitterly admitted that "the history of South Viet-Nam pacification is a list of plans which have collapsed and of talented advisers' boundless efforts which have been reduced to ashes" (AP, January 6, 1967).

The ultimate goal of the limited aggressive war of the U.S. imperialists in South Viet-Nam is to consolidate the puppet army and government and to bring about neocolonialism. However, faced with the fierce conflicts between the U.S. imperialists and lackeys and all our people, and faced with the increasingly strong resistance of the southern people, the internal contradictions of the puppet army and government have developed day by day.

The puppet army and government have daily declined and will surely arrive at complete disintegration and collapse. This actually has happened and is happening in the south of our country. This proves that the U.S. imperialists have sustained heavy defeats on the path leading to the ultimate goal of their neocolonialist aggressive war.

Thus, the American imperialists have been defeated strategically. What about their tactics? It can be said that after waging limited war for two years, they have encountered more and more crises and increasingly greater deadlocks in the tactical field. All their offensive and defensive tactics, as well as all the private tactics of each branch of the U.S. armed forces, have not achieved the expected results.

All forms of tactics—from search-and-destroy, mop-up operations, pacification measures, and rescuing operations to police and security operations, attacks with firepower, chemical poison spraying, and so forth—have proved to be inefficient. The Van Tuoung, Cu Chi, and Plei Me battles as well as the search-and-destroy and mop-up operations during the major campaigns—Five Arrows, Attleboro, Cedar Falls, Junction City, Highway 9, and so forth—have demonstrated the deadlock and failure of these forms of tactics. Modern military bases, such as Da Nang and Chu Lai, and logistic bases, such as Long Binh, Bien Hoa, and so on, have been threatened permanently and attacked repeatedly and have suffered heavy losses. The specific tactics of each American military branch have also been defeated.

Based on the support of armored vehicles, artillery, and aviation, the motorized infantry tactics of the 1st Division has proved inefficient. Faced with the clever tactics of the liberation troops, this tactic of the 1st Division has shown many major weaknesses: one is not free to achieve one's own intention, but must comply with the conditions and tactics of the enemy. The Bau Bang, Cam Xe, Nha Do, Bong Trang, and other battles were bitter defeats for this division.

The Air Cavalry Division's massive heliborne tactics have been aimed at staging surprise raids and swiftly annihilating the enemy. Yet, it has never been able to achieve the surprise factor nor to destroy any section of the LAF. Troops of the Air Cavalry Division are even weaker than ordinary U.S. infantry troops, because they lack the mechanized and artillery support units. Units of the Air Cavalry Division have been battered by the LAF in Plei Me, Binh Dinh, and other localities.

The U.S. Marines' tactics of blocking defense combined with conducting mop-up operations aimed at pacifying areas surrounding military bases has revealed many weaknesses. The Marine bases at Da Nang and Chu Lai are like isolated islands in the open sea of people's war. The Marines, who belong to one of the armed branches regarded by the U.S. imperialists as the most seasoned, have been most frequently and most seriously defeated and are being stretched as taut as a bowstring over hundreds of kilometers in the Tri Thien region and along Highway 9.

The bombing and strafing tactics, which have been aimed at annihilating LAF units, destroying the resistance bases, and massacring the people, have also become ineffective because of inaccurate intelligence information and the failure to identify targets accurately. To date, U.S. Air Force bombings and strafings, including that of B-52 strategic bombers, have not been able to wipe out any LAF unit, but have only, as the U.S. imperialists have often admitted, shattered trees or destroyed empty tunnels.

Why have the various tactics adopted by U.S. troops been ineffective? As everyone knows, tactics are inseparable from strategy. If strategy becomes defensive and stalemated, it will vigorously and adversely affect tactics. The reason for the failure and stalemate of the various tactics adopted by U.S. troops also lies in their erroneous tactical thinking. The American forces' tactics have been based solely upon the power of weapons and upon the assumption that firepower is their soul. Therefore, when these bases—weapons and firepower—are restricted or fail to develop their effectiveness, the tactics become ineffective and are defeated.

The tactics adopted by the U.S. troops in South Viet-Nam are undergoing a crisis and are stalemated, not because they are the outmoded results of a bourgeois military science, but mainly because they cannot match the creative and flexible tactics of the people's war of the heroic, intelligent, valiant, and skillful southern armed forces and people. If American troops were free to fight according to their tactics against an enemy who does not possess fighting experience, their tactics might develop and have a certain effectiveness. Yet, faced with the strength of the people's war and the skillful strategy and tactics of the southern armed forces and people, they have had no freedom of action, and as a result, all their tactics have been ineffective.

The New York Times on February 28, 1967, correctly admitted: "How can they—that is, the American troops—win decisive victories over the South Vietnamese people's armed forces, who cannot be defeated? These armed forces have come from the people and are fighting in areas which are very familiar to them. They know how to apply expertly the art and experiences of the war which they have waged for one-quarter of this century."

The defeat of the U.S. imperialists' tactics and strategies during the past two years on the southern battlefield was very heavy. Although they have poured in more and more troops to set up their limited aggressive war, the U.S. imperialists not only have not achieved their strategic schemes but also have failed to achieve all their strategic goals.

During the past two years, the U.S. imperialists have expanded the war with the aim of discovering a turning point toward victory, but this has eluded them more and more. Moreover, the turning point toward defeat is drawing nearer and nearer for them. Their aggressive war in the south has exceeded the restrictions of a limited war. Yet they are still unable to find a way out. Johnson continues to find that this war is bloody and stalemated. McNamara and Westmoreland are becoming confused and are quarreling with each other about the problems of increasing U.S. strength or of increasing the U.S. troops' fighting efficiency. All the big shots at the White House and Pentagon have admitted that they cannot defeat the adversary. The *Wall Street Journal* on May 20, 1967, said: "In Viet-Nam, the Americans have thrust themselves into a horrible, issueless, eight-diagram battle scheme. It is time to admit that Viet-Nam has become an incurable disease for the Americans."

The experiences drawn from the Viet-Nam war during the past two years have exposed the fallacy of a series of military views held by the American imperialists, as well as of bourgeois military science in general.

The U.S. imperialists maintain that they will surely win if they wage limited war with a large army equipped with modern weapons and supported by the air force and navy. The realities on the Vietnamese battlefield have caused this view to go bankrupt, along with the limited-war theory of the U.S. imperialist aggressors.

First of all, the American imperialists' view that the number of troops decides victory on the battlefield has lost all meaning during the special war as well as the limited war. The Americans and their lackeys have continually had more troops than the southern LAF, but they have never won victory. Facts prove that the U.S. imperialists have been losing on the southern battlefield not because they have lacked troops, and not because their troops have been less numerous than the liberation troops, but because they have encountered an entire nation which has risen up to resist them resolutely, which has had a strongly developed people's war, and which has had a powerful and inexhaustible political force and liberation forces that have a high fighting power and clever tactics.

From the purely numerical viewpoint, it is obvious that over 1 million U.S., puppet, and satellite troops constitute a large force—especially as it is carrying out aggression on a battleground of only 170,000 square kilometers. But to have numerous troops does not necessarily mean to have powerful and efficient fighting power, since their aggressive war is unjust and since they have no fighting spirit and no appropriate tactics and are in a defensive strategic state. The over 1 million U.S., puppet, and satellite troops do not have the hoped-for fighting power.

Along with the argument on troop strength, the argument that equipment and weapons can decide victory has also been smashed.

It can be said that on the southern battlefields, those who have a great amount of up-to-date equipment and weapons are the U.S. imperialists. Except for nuclear weapons, all the most modern weapons and means of war have been lavishly expended. Nevertheless, all this equipment and these weapons have been unable to help the American troops protect themselves and effectively destroy the southern LAF.

Conversely, although they have no aircraft, armored vehicles, or warships, the LAF continues to succeed in destroying U.S., puppet, and satellite troop units equipped with up-to-date equipment.

Everyone knows that armed forces must have equipment and weapons and that these are an important factor in creating fighting strength. However, it is obvious that equipment and weapons are not a factor that can decide victory. What decides victory on the battlefields is whether the armed forces have high fighting spirit and good fighting methods. Only with these can we develop to the fullest extent the use of equipment and weapons in order to defeat the enemy.

The arguments on the strength of the air force and on its use to decide victory on the battlefields has also gone bankrupt. In the south, the U.S. imperialists have a very great superiority in airpower. They have used aircraft, including B-52 strategic bombers, to drop bombs of various types in an attempt to destroy the LAF and massacre the people. However, they continue to be unable to save the U.S. infantry units from defeat and to check the ubiquitous and strong offensive thrust of the southern LAF.

While it is true that the American troops in the south have a considerable air force, it is obvious that the U.S. Air Force's effect has been limited, because it must cope with the widespread people's war of the heroic southern army and people. From Tri Thien to Ca Mau, there are thousands of targets that the Americans want to attack. Therefore, the U.S. Air Force has had to scatter, and, as a result, its fighting effectiveness has not developed as desired. Its failure, from heliborne tactics to large-scale airborne landing tactics, has demonstrated the bankruptcy of the U.S. imperialists' argument concerning airpower on the southern battlefields.

In the north, the U.S. Air Force has been dealt fierce blows. Nearly 2,300 up-to-date fighter aircraft of various types have been destroyed in the northern skies. The American air superiority has disastrously collapsed.

U.S. aircraft, bombs, and bullets cannot intimidate our

people. McNamara himself acknowledged that bombs and bullets cannot weaken North Viet-Nam. This is an acknowledgment of the inefficiency of the U.S. Air Force in the American imperialists' war of aggression in Viet-Nam.

The limited-war strategy is collapsing along with the unimaginable strength of the U.S. armed forces. The war is not ended. However, it can be concluded that the American limited-war strategy in the south has proved inefficient and will certainly meet with complete failure. In the unjust war of aggression in Viet-Nam, the U.S. expeditionary troops, with nearly 500,000 men with modern equipment, have not won any victory and are nothing but a defeated armed force.

In war, the ground forces play a decisive role on the battlefields. Nevertheless, the fighting strength of American ground forces is very poor, their morale is lower than grass, and their fighting methods are bad. The U.S. generals are subjective and haughty and have always been caught by surprise and defeated.

The U.S. imperialists have spent much effort to publicize the so-called unimaginable strength of their armed forces, with the aim of intimidating the world's people —especially the people of small and weak nations. This trick has failed. The truth is that the American expeditionary troops are being defeated in the people's war of the Vietnamese, who, although not possessing a vast territory and not having a great population, rely mainly on their own strength and are determined to fight in order to wrest back independence and freedom.

PART

*The People Throughout
the Country Have Achieved
Very Great Victories*

The foregoing is a review of the heavy setbacks, especially strategic and tactical, of the U.S. imperialists, in implementing the strategy of aggressive limited war in South Viet-Nam during the past two years. For our people, the past two anti-U.S., national salvation years were violent fighting and testing years, during which they have achieved very great and glorious victories.

Confronted with the fact that the American imperialists have sent massive expeditionary troops to South Viet-Nam and frenziedly stepped up the war of destruction, mainly by means of their air and naval forces, against the north, the people in the entire country find themselves in a very serious situation; that is, in a struggle for the country's survival. This situation sets forth for our people throughout the country a common duty: to unite the entire people and make both north and south stand shoulder to shoulder in intensifying the great patriotic war and in being determined to fight to vanquish the U.S. aggressors in order to protect the north, liberate the south, and advance toward the unification of the fatherland.

President Ho has said: "At present, struggling against U.S. aggression and for national salvation is the most sacred duty of every patriotic Vietnamese. All our soldiers and people are united and of the same mind, fear no sacrifices and hardships, and are determined to fight until complete victory."

On the South Viet-Nam battlefield, with their special-war strategy going bankrupt, the U.S. imperialists have been forced to shift to the limited-war strategy. However, the character of their war still is one of aggression aimed at achieving the political objectives of neocolonialism. Thus, their war is a neocolonialist aggressive war.

The anti-U.S., national salvation resistance fight of the Vietnamese people in South Viet-Nam is a revolutionary war, a people's war developed to an unprecedentedly high degree. It is a revolutionary struggle, a people's war of an entire people against American imperialism's neo-colonialist aggressive war.

The great resistance war is developing favorably, because it is directed by an accurate and creative line and because it has synthetically applied and creatively developed all the valuable experiences and forms of struggle of the Vietnamese revolution, ranging from the political to uprisings and war. Thus our people's anti-U.S., national salvation resistance war is progressing according to all the laws of a revolutionary war against a neo-colonialist aggressive one—laws, whose main contents are the spirit of indomitable struggle of a heroic people, the spirit of thorough revolution of the working class and the basic masses of workers and peasants, and the skillful and unique combination of all forms of struggle, especially of the political with the armed struggle, in all regions of the country, from jungles, rural areas, and plains to cities.

Naturally under the direction of all these laws, each form of struggle, such as the armed and the political struggles, has its own law. Since our people are already equipped with an indomitable spirit—better to die than agree to serve as slaves—have at their disposal very valuable revolutionary experiences, hold fast to the laws of revolutionary war against neocolonialist aggressive war, have very correct strategies and tactics, understand the enemy and friendly situations, and are resolved and know how to fight to defeat the enemy, their anti-U.S., national salvation resistance war has achieved great victories and will certainly achieve final victory.

Grasping the character and goal of the U.S. imperialists' limited war, our people in South Viet-Nam continue to develop their achievements, strive to step up the people's war, and are resolved to fight and vanquish the American aggressors. The strategies and tactics of the people's war have undergone new developments, so that they are consistent with the new conditions of the war.

The southern armed forces and people have asserted that their combat targets are the American and puppet forces. These are the enemy's strategic forces used to prosecute the war of aggression. They rely on each other and fight in close cooperation. The U.S. troops are the core forces, which is a military buttress for the puppet armed forces and administration and at the same time the main mobile force. The fact that they are heavily defeated will have a very great adverse effect on the puppet armed forces and administration, causing the puppet troops to disintegrate and the puppet administration to collapse quickly. Since the U.S. armed forces are the most modern armed forces in the capitalist world, they need abundant war means and important logistic bases. Therefore, we seek to destroy not only American military strength but also the enemy's war means and logistic bases.

The puppet armed forces rely on the U.S. forces to survive and to consolidate and develop their ranks. But they play a very important role toward the Americans in the neocolonialist aggressive war. They are the political buttress for the American forces. They are used as both occupation forces and mobile forces on the battlefields. They are primarily in charge of controlling and oppressing the people and at the same time of carrying out the pacification task. The fact that they are destroyed and disintegrated will deprive the U.S. forces of a support for continuing their neocolonialist aggressive war.

The puppet administration is the political buttress and an instrument for the U.S. imperialists to achieve neocolonialism. In view of this, our people in South Viet-Nam have combined their armed struggle with political struggle, in order to overthrow the puppet administration not only at the basic level, as they have done so far, but also at other levels.

By clearly acknowledging their combat targets, our people in South Viet-Nam have correctly and successfully settled the strategic and tactical problems of the people's war. They have waged an all-people, comprehensive, and protracted resistance war in which they have always taken the offensive, have relied on their own force, which they consider as the principal force, and have highly appreciated the support of brother socialist countries and progressive people all over the world. The resistance war of our people will certainly be victorious, even though it calls forth sacrifices and hardships.

The participation of all our people in the anti-U.S., national salvation resistance war is one of the basic points in our country's people's-war strategy. The objective of our southern compatriots' resistance war is to liberate the south, defend the north, and advance toward the reunification of the fatherland. This objective is entirely consistent with the profound aspirations of all people. This has been instrumental in mobilizing and organizing all people to take part in the anti-U.S., national salvation resistance war, thus forming a large and strong resistance force in which 14 million South Vietnamese people are combatants, fighting the enemy by all means and everywhere.

Since the victory of the general uprising, the South Viet-Nam NLF has developed and broadened the great national unity bloc, has succeeded in mobilizing all people to stand up to save the country and themselves, and has insured the practical interests of the people in all walks of life, including the peasants' right to own land. Therefore, the front has been able to consolidate the worker-peasant alliance as a firm and steady foundation for the great national united front against U.S. aggression and for national salvation.

Ever since the sending of American troops to invade South Viet-Nam, the conflicts between the U.S. imperialists and the country-selling Vietnamese traitors and the Vietnamese people have become increasingly acute and deep. Our people in South Viet-Nam, millions as one, have closed their ranks in the all-people unity bloc under the NLF's invincible banner in order to fight U.S. aggression and to save the country. Since our people in South Viet-Nam have carried out the slogan of "All people are armed and take part in fighting the enemy," the people's war has been developed deeply and broadly and has produced a great effect.

On the basis of the participation of all people in the anti-U.S., national salvation resistance war, our people in South Viet-Nam have built and developed swiftly the liberation armed forces which are composed of three kinds of troops: the guerrillas, the regional units, and the main force units. These three kinds of troops of the liberation armed forces are a core force of the southern people in their anti-U.S., national salvation resistance war. With a large political force and with increasingly large and strong liberation forces, the South Vietnamese people will certainly and completely defeat more than 1 million U.S., puppet, and satellite troops.

In our country, at present, fighting against U.S. aggression and for national salvation is the great, sacred historic task of the Vietnamese people as a whole. Our people in the south and the north resolutely stand together in fighting until final victory in order to achieve independence and freedom for the entire country. Waging a comprehensive resistance war is a very important strategic problem for developing our strength in all fields in order to vanquish the aggressors, an enemy with numerous troops and strong equipment, but with many contradictions and weaknesses in its neocolonialist war of aggression.

A striking characteristic of the people's war in our country at present is that even within the limited war, the fight against the enemy on all fronts—military, political, cultural, diplomatic, and so forth—is waged at the same time, in which the military and the political struggles are the most basic forms of struggle. The military and political struggles are closely coordinated, assist each other, and encourage each other to develop. This coordination is a law of the revolutionary struggle in our country. It is also an initiative of our people in the process of the protracted revolutionary war.

The political struggle plays a very important role throughout the anti-U.S., national salvation resistance. In our country, the political struggle of the masses has always served as a basis for the development of the military struggle. At present in South Viet-Nam, our people's struggle has become a direct confrontation with the enemy, and together with the military struggle, has scored repeated and great successes.

In the present limited warfare, the political struggle continues to play a very important role. The U.S. imperialists have used expeditionary forces to launch direct aggression against South Viet-Nam. But they are forced to carry out a neocolonialist policy, and to resort to all kinds of political maneuvers to fool the people. This constitutes an opportunity for the South Vietnamese people to further intensify their political struggle. Moreover, the sending of American troops to launch direct aggression against South Viet-Nam has further developed the conflicts between our people and the U.S. imperialists. Therefore, the South Vietnamese people of all walks of life, including those who did not realize the true nature of the U.S. aggressors or who were fooled into following them, have now stood up to fight the enemy. This constitutes a favorable condition for the South Vietnamese people's struggle to develop and to score great victories.

The main objectives of the political struggle are to mobilize and organize the people, to guide them in the struggle against the enemy in all ways, and at the same time closely to coordinate with the military struggle and to help it win the greatest victories for the resistance.

The more violent the war becomes, the more strengthened and effective the political struggle will be, especially in the urban centers of South Viet-Nam where many conflicts exist between the U.S. imperialists and their henchmen on the one hand and our people on the other, and where there are contradictions even among the U.S. imperialists, and so forth. In the process of the anti-U.S., national salvation resistance, the political struggle of our urban compatriots of South Viet-Nam will play an ever more important role and directly hit the enemy in their deepest dens.

The military struggle is becoming even more important and is playing a decisive role directly in defeating the enemy on the battlefield. At present the U.S. imperialists are concentrating their forces and resorting to a policy of arms and force to invade South Viet-Nam and enslave our people. Therefore, our people in South Viet-Nam have to resort to revolutionary violence to oppose the counterrevolutionary violence and to use military struggle to oppose the armed aggression of the enemy. The U.S. imperialists are using a huge military force to carry out aggression in South Viet-Nam. As a result, the military struggle of our people in the south has become ever more important.

The main objectives of the military struggle are to destroy the enemy military force, to defend the people, to attract the people's sympathy, to coordinate with the political struggle, and to serve and help the political struggle score the greatest victories for the resistance.

Along with the political struggle, the military one of our people in South Viet-Nam has defeated over 500,000 puppet troops in the special war and is now defeating over 1 million U.S., puppet, and satellite troops in the limited war. In parallel with the new progress of the political struggle, the military struggle of the South Vietnamese people has developed and is developing strongly, quickly, and steadfastly in both forms, guerrilla and large-scale combat.

Guerrilla activities and large-scale combat coordinate with each other, help each other, and encourage each other to develop. At the same time, they closely coordinate with the political struggle to gain great victories in both military and political fields, thus leading the resistance toward final victory. Protracted resistance is an essential strategy of a people of a country which is neither large nor too populous and which has restricted economic and military potentials, but who are determined to defeat an enemy and aggressor having large and well-armed forces.

The anti-U.S., national salvation resistance of our people in South Viet-Nam must be a protracted resistance, because our people have to fight the imperialists' ringleaders, that is, the U.S. imperialists, who have large military and economic potentials. Despite their bitter defeats, the enemy is still very obdurate. In the process of their protracted resistance, the longer they fight, the stronger the South Vietnamese people become; while the longer the enemy fights, the greater difficulties he encounters. The comparison of forces on the battlefields turns in our people's favor and creates favorable conditions for them to rush ahead and completely to defeat the enemy. In carrying out their protracted resistance, the South Vietnamese people have frustrated the *blitzkrieg* strategic scheme of the U.S. aggressor and forced him to fight in accordance with our strategy, thus causing him to be extremely confused and incapable of escaping complete defeat.

In the present era, with the common offensive thrust of the world revolution, national liberation wars have favorable conditions for developing. National liberation wars can and will certainly score victories without necessarily being connected with a world war or with the revolution right in the country of the imperialist aggressors. Therefore, national liberation wars must allow some time, and a long time, to be able to crush the aggressive desire of the colonialist imperialists and to win final victory.

Our people greatly appreciate the struggle of the American people against the aggressive Viet-Nam war of the Johnson Administration, considering it a valuable mark of sympathy and support of our people's just resistance. Moreover, our people are thoroughly aware that the decisive factor for the success of the anti-U.S., national salvation resistance is their objective efforts to turn the balance of forces more and more in our favor on the Viet-Nam battlefield, where there is a firm struggle between the aggressors and the victims of aggression, and where the war situation is developing more and more in favor of the heroic South Vietnamese people.

Our people hold that after forthcoming Presidential elections in the United States, and despite a possible change of Presidents, the U.S. imperialists' aggressive policy cannot be changed in nature. The U.S. Presidential elections constitute but a distributing of hierarchies among the personalities of the parties of the ruling capitalist class in the United States. Of course, through the forthcoming elections, the American people will better realize the errors and setbacks of the Johnson Administration in the aggressive war in Viet-Nam. And so, the struggle of the American people against the aggressive war will be stronger.

The southern people's strategy of protracted fighting

reflects the determination to fight and the ability of our people to defeat the U.S. imperialists under all war circumstances. The southern people, as well as the people in our entire country, are ready to carry on the resistance for five, ten, twenty, or more years, and are firmly confident of victory. In the protracted resistance against the U.S. imperialist aggressors, our people in the south are able and determined to gain time and to score increasingly greater achievements. The southern people are able to do this, because in the past they have scored great achievements and because the resistance forces have swiftly matured.

On this basis, the southern army and people will make greater efforts and will certainly have greater and greater achievements. They are able to do this, because the U.S. imperialists, following their successive, heavy setbacks, are driven into a strategically deadlocked situation, the U.S. troops' fighting efficiency has continuously decreased, they are considerably scattered and defensive, and the puppet troops and administration are on the verge of collapse. The U.S. ruling circles have been increasingly opposed by the American people and are being isolated politically to a high degree in the international arena.

Although it is great, the U.S. economic and military potential is not boundless. Moreover, the realities of the war in Viet-Nam have proved that although they have a great number of troops, good rifles, and much money, the Americans are unable to extricate themselves from defeat and deadlock and will certainly be completely defeated.

Relying mainly on our own force but at the same time

seeking assistance from the socialist bloc and the people of the world is a very important strategic matter. This is a manifestation of the masses' steadfast viewpoint, which places absolute confidence in our people and nation, who are imbued with an indomitable tradition and have sufficient circumstances and ability to defeat the aggressive enemy, even if it is the U.S. imperialists.

Revolution is the work of the masses. No one can replace our people in carrying out the resistance to wrest back independence and freedom for the Vietnamese fatherland. Only our people can decide their destiny. Relying mainly on our own force and the all-people united strength, and firmly grasping the strategy and tactics of the invincible people's war, our people are determined to defeat the aggressive enemy, the U.S. imperialists.

Relying mainly on their own force, our people have defeated hundreds of thousands of professional troops of the French aggressor colonialists. Relying mainly on their own force, our people in the south have successfully conducted a general uprising and have defeated the special war of the Americans and the puppets. Relying mainly on their own force, they have defeated the first phase of the U.S. imperialists' limited-war strategy and will certainly and completely defeat more than 1 million U.S., puppet, and satellite troops.

The present time is the era of revolutionary storms. The strong socialist bloc is becoming a factor which decides the development of human society, and the people's liberation movement is boiling throughout Asia, Africa, and Latin America. Imperialism, headed by the U.S. imperialists, is being repeatedly attacked everywhere;

our people can and must fully develop the advantages of the present era and positively seek assistance from the socialist countries and the people in the world in order to strengthen our force and ability to defeat the U.S. imperialist aggressors.

Our people do not divorce our anti-U.S., national salvation resistance from the present era and highly value the assistance of the socialist countries and our friends in the world. Nevertheless, relying mainly on our own force must be accepted as a matter of primary and decisive importance. In the southern part of our country, the offensive strategy is the strategy of the people's war in the anti-U.S., national salvation resistance.

In the south, the offensive strategy has been carried out by our people since the general uprising period, and the coordinated military and political offensive strategy has scored great achievements in defeating the enemy's special war. Nevertheless, when the U.S. imperialists sent in masses of troops directly to invade the south, the problem was whether our people would continue to carry out the offensive strategy. The southern people have continued to do so, because their resistance constitutes a winning position and because the southern people also possess mature military and political forces, which create conditions for further swift development, while the U.S. imperialists and their lackeys are being heavily defeated and are seriously declining. At the outset, the U.S. expeditionary troops introduced into the south were forced to remain in a strategically passive and scattered position in order to cope with the people's war, which has developed vigorously everywhere.

The striking characteristic of the offensive strategy

of our southern people is to attack comprehensively and continuously and to gain the initiative in attacking the enemy everywhere with all forces and weapons and with all appropriate methods. The comprehensive offensive is a coordinated military and political offensive and includes the attacks on U.S. troops and the puppet troops and administration in the mountains and jungle areas, the deltas, and the cities. This requires a very great determination and very flexible, creative attack methods. Our people have succeeded in doing this, because they have an extremely valiant fighting spirit, mature political and armed forces, and unique, versatile, and extremely damaging fighting methods.

The southern people have used all means of the military and political struggles to attack the enemy. It is due to coordinated military and political attacks on the enemy that their offensive strategy has acquired strong and great effect. It is due to the fact that the offensive strategy has been carried out in a flexible and creative manner, depending upon the place, time, and objective, that the southern people have developed a very steadfast offensive strategic posture and have driven the enemy deep into an embattled and defensive position everywhere. Not only have the armed forces, including the three categories of guerrillas, regional forces, and regular troops, carried out the offensive strategy, but the women's troops, and all the people in the political forces have also repeatedly attacked the enemy.

It is on the basis of this offensive strategy that the revolutionary war in the south, with its various forms, has successfully developed and has acquired greater strength. It is on the basis of this offensive strategy that the people's army and political struggles have developed successfully from the rural areas to the cities and from the mountains and jungle areas to the deltas, and especially on the battlefields and in various strategic directions. These creative forms of struggle, including the political struggle with its extremely rich contents, from low level to high, and the armed struggle, from guerrilla warfare to attacks with concentrated forces and with skilled, flexible, and unique fighting methods, have allowed the people's armed and political forces to develop their offensive strength to a high degree and attack the areas regarded by the enemy as indestructible, thus opening extremely great new prospects and capabilities for the offensive strategy and giving it—a comprehensive and continuous offensive—an immeasurable strength, an invincible strength.

The foregoing is a summary of the main contents of the people's-war strategy, which our southern people have applied in the present anti-U.S., national salvation resistance. This strategy has achieved very great victories and has defeated the limited-war strategy of the U.S. imperialists during its recent very important phase.

The "all people resist the Americans for national salvation" strategy has caused the large and strong U.S., puppet, and satellite forces of more than 1 million men to become small and weak. Comprehensive resistance has made the already defensive enemy become more defensive in all fields. The strategy of protracted resistance has defeated the *blitzkrieg* strategy of the U.S. imperialists and their lackeys. The offensive strategy has developed to a high level the great political and military power of the entire nation and driven more than 1 million enemy troops into a defensive and embattled state.

It is obvious that our people's-war strategy is superior to all strategies of the U.S. imperialist aggressors. Every day it has proved that it is invincible. To defeat the American imperialists, our people have not only correct, creative, and very effective strategies, but also clever tactics.

We all know that with good tactics a certain number of troops can defeat the enemy, but if the tactics are bad, these troops can hardly be victorious and sometimes sustain losses. In war, to defeat the enemy's strategies and open the way for greater victories, it is sometimes better to fight a few battles with good tactics than to fight many battles with bad tactics. In fighting an enemy having millions of troops, we will encounter many difficulties if we do not have flexible and creative tactics. If we have good tactics, not only can we achieve great results in fighting, but also develop the effectiveness of military operations and strategies and deal heavy blows to the enemy aggressors.

In the south of our country, by strongly developing the people's-war strategy, the LAF has heightened the wonderful courage, resourcefulness, creativeness, and spirit of mastery; developed to a high degree the efficiency of all weapons at hand; limited the efficiency of the enemy's modern weapons; and invented clever, varied, and effective tactics.

All tactics of the LAF have been invented and developed on the basis of intense patriotism, deep hatred for the foe, and the spirit of voluntarily, actively, and resolutely finding resourceful and creative means to attack and destroy the enemy.

On the southern battlefield, the tactics of the guerrilla force have developed in varied ways, thus greatly frightening the enemy. The guerrillas have fought with primitive weapons such as spikes, mines, and traps, as well as with semimodern and modern weapons. They have fought with means aimed at decimating as well as annihilating the enemy. The guerrillas have recognized the enemy's weak points and fully developed their own strong points.

They have discovered clever tactics and devoted their courage, spirit of sacrifice, and intelligence to carrying them out successfully. Now the southern guerrillas' tactics are very powerful.

There have been battles in which guerrillas have defeated raids by enemy battalions, in which a guerrilla squad annihilated an entire U.S. company, in which guerrillas have destroyed an enemy command headquarters. Cases of shooting at and burning the enemy's armored vehicles, planes, warships, and so forth have become common among southern guerrillas. Southern guerrillas have stretched out the enemy to decimate and destroy him, thus sowing great fear in his ranks.

On the southern battlefield, the LAF's method of fighting with concentrated forces to annihilate completely enemy troops has increasingly evolved and has been very effective. On the basis of the people's war, which has developed to a high degree, and in coordination with the guerrilla and regional forces, the LAF's main-force units have dealt powerful blows on all battlefields.

With gallantry and skill and by restricting to a minimum the effect of the enemy's aircraft and artillery, fully developing all kinds of weapons, and deepening the difficulties encountered by U.S. troops—low morale, unfamiliarity with the terrain and climate, poor command, and so forth—the southern LAF has dealt serious, destructive blows to the enemy, whether he remains in his well-fortified and adequately protected bases, or moves out to launch attacks or conduct mop-up operations, and even if he belongs to seasoned U.S. divisions, such as the 1st Infantry Division, the Air Cavalry Division, U.S. Marine divisions, and so forth.

Attacking U.S. military bases and logistical installations is also a powerful fighting method of the LAF on the southern battlefield. Although the enemy stays deep in his extremely well-protected bases, the LAF has been able to penetrate far into his lairs, inflict very heavy losses on him, and, as the enemy has admitted, has carried the fear of war to his bed.

LAF attacks against the U.S. bases at Da Nang and Chu Lai, the large airfields, and the logistical installations at Lien Chieu, Long Binh, and many other areas have brought about very great results, which were like the feats of arms scored by a marvelous strategic air force unit of the people's war and which, as the enemy has had to admit, could not be prevented or warded off.

On the southern battlefield the LAF's method of attacking cities is being developed. With the support of the people's political forces, small units of the LAF have succeeded in winning resounding victories and destroying a substantial part of the enemy's viability. In particular, the attacks launched by the LAF in the heart of

Saigon, Hue, and other cities have supported the struggle movement of the urban compatriots, frightened the foe, and filled the hearts of our compatriots throughout the country with elation. The attacks on the cities have demonstrated the marvelous courage, skill, and flexibility of the LAF.

On the southern battlefields, the LAF methods for attacking military communications, especially important strategic axes of communications, are very effective. With them, the LAF has disrupted and paralyzed the enemy's ground logistical supply movement and weakened his mobility on the battlefields. The U.S. and puppet troops were forced to shift an important part of their forces to protect and clear their communications, but to date the enemy's military communications still face many difficulties, and his important strategic routes are still constantly and violently attacked and threatened.

The LAF's methods for attacking military communications are becoming more effective, thus making it impossible for the U.S. expeditionary troops to develop the effectiveness of their up-to-date equipment and high mobility. At present, in the south, all three categories of troops—guerrillas, regional forces, and regular troops—are very familiar with the methods for attacking military communications and are placing the U.S. and puppet troops in a truly perilous situation on the military communications front.

On the southern battlefields, the LAF forces also have other skillful fighting methods, such as those designed to destroy enemy positions, to combine fighting with troop proselytizing in order to disintegrate the enemy ranks, to combine fighting with military revolt in order to destroy one important unit of the enemy after another, to combine political struggle with military struggle in order to destroy strategic hamlets, to foment revolts in the rural areas, and so forth.

In the process of fighting and defeating the U.S., puppet, and satellite troops, our southern people have constantly sought fighting methods that are able to help develop the strength of all their military and political forces to a high degree with a view continuously and comprehensively to attack the enemy at all times and in all places, defeat all his strategies and tactics, and win increasingly greater achievements.

At present these fighting methods of the LAF have been creatively and effectively applied by the three categories of troops: guerrillas, regional forces, and regular troops. Herewith, I present only the fighting methods adopted by the LAF's main-force units and which have undergone development.

Fighting methods are based upon coordination among various armed branches and the independent method of each. The coordinated fighting method of different armed branches of the LAF is one in which infantry troops constitute the main elements operating in coordination with one or many other armed branches and creating a superior strength and a powerful fighting capacity in order to annihilate major units or command posts of the enemy.

Because of the characteristics of the situation of friendly and enemy units on the battlefield, the organization of coordinated fighting does not depend on the availability of units of all armed branches. The LAF has proceeded from coordinating combat among a few armed branches toward coordinating combat among many, on the basis of using infantry troops as the main elements, with a view to developing the decisive role of infantry on the battlefield.

Thus, to improve the effectiveness of the coordinated fighting method, the LAF has attached great importance to building and developing many infantry units which fight effectively under all circumstances by coordinating their actions with the armed branches and by combining many fighting methods and tactical forms and tricks of the people's war.

In addition to the fighting method based upon co-ordination among various armed branches, with infantry units constituting the main elements, the LAF has also adopted fighting methods based upon coordination among the various armed branches themselves. For instance, coordination between artillery units and crack special units, between engineer and anti-aircraft units, and so forth. The existing conditions and the nature of the need to annihilate the enemy serve as a basis for determining the coordination of combat between this armed branch and the other, with a view to adopting a fighting method able to insure victory and rapid and complete annihilation of enemy troops.

To insure that the fighting method based upon co-ordination among various armed branches achieves increasing effectiveness, the southern liberation forces have laid special emphasis on developing the highest efficiency in the use of all kinds of weapons and equipment, developing to a high degree the liberation troops' fighting ability, and using each unit and each armed branch at the right time and place, with a view to raising its level of mastery over the battlefield and completely destroying large enemy units.

The liberation forces' fighting methods based upon coordination is being vigorously promoted along with the steady development of the armed branches, especially that of the infantry units, and in accordance with the growing requirement for concentrated fighting. The fighting method based upon coordination among various armed branches will certainly make a decisive contribution toward annihilating many large units and many important bases of the enemy, changing the situation on the battlefield in favor of the southern people and providing them with opportunities to move forward to defeat completely more than 1 million troops of the U.S. imperialist aggressors.

The method of independent fighting by each armed branch is a very unique creation of the people's war in the southern part of our country. Aside from the infantry force, the other armed branches of the liberation armed forces, such as the artillery units, the crack special units, the engineer units, the anti-aircraft units, and so forth, have their fighting methods. The common characteristic of the independent fighting methods adopted by various armed branches is the thorough comprehension of the spirit of positively attacking and annihilating the enemy, developing to the highest degree the fighting ability of each armed branch, and contributing toward developing the initiative of the southern armed forces and people at any time, anywhere, and in the face of any enemy. With the method of independent fighting of various armed branches, the southern LAF has succeeded in creating many opportunities to attack the enemy and in enabling the armed branches to acquire a tremendous new fighting ability.

The method of independent fighting by the artillery units of the LAF is:

On the southern battlefield today, the LAF's artillery units, by fighting in coordination with infantry units as well as independently, have increasingly developed their tremendous power. In many separately fought battles, the LAF's artillery units have rapidly annihilated a substantial part of the enemy troops just as they began to maneuver or assemble. The LAF's artillery barrages against the enemy's command posts, military bases, and logistical installations as well as against his bivouacs have inflicted heavy losses and rendered the enemy panic-stricken. It goes without saying that for the artillery units, independent fighting is but one method. The primary mission of artillery units is to fight in coordination with infantry units and to support the infantry in major battles in order to annihilate large enemy units.

The method of independent fighting by the crack special units, whose numbers are small but whose quality is high, has achieved extremely great results. No matter where the enemy troops are located and no matter how adequately protected they may be, regardless of whether they are U.S. or puppet troops or whether they are in airbases, logistical facilities, U.S. officers' quarters, and so forth, with their independent fighting method, the LAF's crack special units have been able to harm them seriously. With boundless courage, marvelous intelligence, and a thoroughly tested fighting capacity, the special units, with their own fighting methods, have dealt vigorous surprise blows at the enemy and rendered him incapable of reacting in time. With small numbers but high quality, they have defeated the enemy and inflicted heavy losses on him even in areas where large infantry or artillery units have encountered difficulties in organizing combat. The independent fighting method of the crack special units is developing vigorously among the three categories of troops. This has created new fighting abilities and strength for the LAF to annihilate increasingly large numbers of the enemy's military forces everywhere.

With their methods of independent fighting, the LAF engineering units have paralyzed the enemy's communications, cut the important strategic routes, destroyed military bridges, attacked the enemy's mechanized vehicles, and so forth. They have inflicted very serious losses on the foe. Of course, the engineering units also have the primary task of supporting the infantry and the artillery units in combat. Yet, with their independent methods, engineering units have contributed toward effectively destroying the enemy in a situation in which the LAF is fighting against U.S. troops, who possess plenty of modern weapons and instruments.

With their methods of independent fighting, the LAF's anti-aircraft units have inflicted considerable losses on the enemy's air force and have restricted to a minimum the activities of his aircraft, especially his helicopters. Although they are newly developed units, the LAF's anti-aircraft units have demonstrated a courageous fighting spirit and resourcefulness and have created fighting methods which are appropriate for the southern battlefields. As a result, they have inflicted considerable losses on the enemy and have caused many difficulties for him in developing the effectiveness of his air force on the southern battlefield. The southern LAF's anti-aircraft units have increasingly matured in combat and will certainly deal more serious blows to the U.S. Air Force.

The fighting method based upon coordination among various armed branches and the methods of independent fighting of each branch of the LAF have indicated that the liberation forces know how to apply the universal principle of concentrating forces to annihilate the enemy and, at the same time, know how to apply the principle of using a small number of troops to defeat a large number of enemy troops who possess modern equipment.

This fact indicates another invention of the people's war and the Vietnamese military art: Not only in the strategic field do we use a small force against a larger force, but in the tactical field, along with using a large force to strike at a smaller force, we use a small force against a larger force. Events on the South Viet-Nam battlefield have proved that this fighting method is completely and definitely feasible and has been fruitfully implemented. Naturally, when the tactics of using a small force to fight a large force is applied, we must have the following conditions: the quality of units must be high; the targets must be chosen carefully; opportunities must be created and the situation maintained, especially when there are flaws acquired by the enemy; actions must be unexpected and swift; and so forth.

With such varied and creative fighting methods, the South Viet-Nam LAF has been able to strike at all targets, in and outside fortifications, to destroy both the enemy's strength and war means, and to attack even his military headquarters and bases, logistic bases, communi-

cation lines, cities, and so forth, thus inflicting heavy
damage on enemy forces in all domains and everywhere.

With these methods, especially that of coordinated
fighting among various armed branches, not only has the
South Viet-Nam LAF taken the initiative in counterattacking and smashing the enemy's counteroffensive
strategy, but it has also continuously attacked the enemy,
achieved glorious victories, and greatly developed its
offensive posture on all battlefronts, in jungle and mountain areas, in rural areas, and in the cities. These fighting
methods, have enabled the liberation forces to develop
to a high degree their militant strength, permitting their
three categories of troops to develop their strong offensive force. Not only have the main-force units adopted
the method of coordinated fighting among various armed
branches, but the regional and guerrilla forces are also
advancing toward the adoption of this method. As a result of their being closely combined with the means of
the political struggle, these varied and creative fighting
methods have become increasingly strong and effective
and have brought about resounding victories on battlefields.

A very important factor deciding the victories of the
liberation forces in all battles is their skillful and creative
fighting techniques. Although the U.S. forces have
fought many battles, they have not achieved victories
because their methods have been clumsy. The fighting
methods of the South Vietnamese armed forces and people prevail over those of the U.S., puppet, and satellite
forces. They are the techniques of a creative people's
war and a brave, heroic, unyielding, intelligent, and resourceful people who, though living in a small and less

populous country, possess a steadfast determination to fight to protect their fatherland and are resolved and know how to defeat the U.S. imperialist aggressors' armed forces, consisting of more than 1 million men.

We have just dealt with how the strategies and tactics of the South Vietnamese people's war have defeated those of the limited war of the U.S. imperialists and their lackeys. But besides the problems of strategies and tactics, there is another very basic problem: How many troops do our people need to defeat the U.S. imperialists' aggressive armed forces of more than 1 million men? Our people in South Viet-Nam have settled this problem very satisfactorily and successfully.

Based on the development of the people's war, our people in the south have attached importance to the building of military and political forces, considering it a decisive factor in implementing the strategies and tactics of the people's war. Our people in South Viet-Nam, under the glorious banner of the NLF, have developed the experiences of the former resistance war against the French and have been able to evolve a policy on the building of armed and political forces, a policy which is consistent with the present conditions of the anti-U.S., national salvation resistance war.

Although South Viet-Nam is not large and is less populous, our southern compatriots have been able to build strong military and political forces that have great militant strength and are fully capable of vanquishing more than 1 million U.S., puppet, and satellite troops who have modern equipment. This armed forces–building policy consists of mobilizing and arming all people and urging them to participate in the war in which the armed forces serve as a nucleus. It is a policy of constructing the armed forces, composed of three categories of troops, along with creating increasingly large and broad political forces of the people.

Concerning the building of the military forces, our people in the south maintain that to develop the people's war to a high degree and to step up the armed struggle, it is necessary to pay attention to the creation of three categories of troops. It is necessary to build both steady, strong, widespread self-defense, guerrilla forces, and main-force units.

The building and development of the regional forces and main-force units must conform to the practical conditions of each region and of the battlefield. These concentrated armed forces must in fact constitute the core groups in annihilating the enemy's military units, protecting the people, and achieving increasingly greater successes. The main-force units must not necessarily possess a strength equaling that of the enemy, but their quality must be high and their fighting methods must be highly effective so that they can deal steel-like blows to the enemy. They must be fully capable of fighting big annihilating battles, dealing serious blows to the enemy, and changing the situation on the battlefield in our favor. Today the southern people's three categories of troops—guerrilla, regional, and main-force units— have developed harmoniously. They have been rationally deployed on various battlefields, have increasingly developed their great fighting strength, and have been able to enhance their position and improve the strategic effect of the LAF in the anti-U.S., national salvation struggle.

The LAF has been fighting while building up its

strength and has unceasingly improved its fighting quality. Along with intensifying political education and military training, adequate attention has been paid to improving equipment, weapons, and combat instruments. As a result, all three categories of troops have acquired a greater fighting strength and will certainly deal more vigorous blows to the enemy.

With regard to building political forces, the southern people have satisfactorily settled the relations between developing their political forces numerically and constantly improving their quality by broadening the all-people's great united bloc and firmly consolidating the key role of the worker-peasant alliance. Today, the southern people's political forces are very numerous and powerful. It is fitting to say that the 14 million southerners are closing their ranks and moving forward to attack the enemy through both military and political struggle.

The political corps, which constitutes the core elements of the people's political struggle movement, has been strengthened both quantitatively and qualitatively and has vigorously developed in the cities as well as in the rural and mountainous areas.

The political forces of the people in southern cities and towns have developed more and more comprehensively and will certainly further intensify their political struggle and continuous attacks against the enemy's lairs. The southern people's armed and political forces have been built along a correct and creative line. As a result, they have acquired a tremendous strength, which serves as a basis for stepping up the people's war, have closely coordinated armed with political struggle, have achieved extremely great successes, and will certainly defeat totally the U.S. imperialists' war of aggression and overthrow the puppet administration.

If in South Viet-Nam our armed forces and people under the NLF's leadership have achieved great victories during the past two years, in North Viet-Nam our armed forces and people, under the leadership of the party, government, and respected and beloved President Ho, have defeated the U.S. imperialists' war of destruction and frustrated their basic schemes while, at the same time, continuing to build socialism and wholeheartedly to support the liberation struggle of our kith and kin, our southern compatriots. We have mobilized and organized all people to participate in resisting the war of destruction by positively fighting the enemy and positively engaging in people's air defense.

In the field of positively fighting the U.S. air and naval forces, we have mobilized all people to fight, using the armed forces as a nucleus. We have simultaneously marshaled and organized all people to participate in shooting down U.S. aircraft and have strengthened the anti-aircraft defense forces, the coast guard forces, and the frontier and demarcation-line defense forces. While developing the capacity of all armed branches and of the regional and the self-defense and militia forces to fight U.S. aircraft, we have strengthened our anti-aircraft defense, air forces, and artillery forces and improved their technical and tactical standards.

We have greatly developed the effect of anti-aircraft guns and other ordinary types of infantry weapons, while striving to develop the effectiveness of jet fighter planes and anti-aircraft missiles in order to create thick and highly effective fire nets. While fighting, we have carried out training and drawn from our fighting experiences in order to improve the quality of anti-aircraft defense of our armed forces. We have positively resisted the enemy's planes and warships, while improving our combat activity, and stand ready to fight and defeat the enemy when he ventures to expand the limited war to the north.

The principle of combat adopted by our armed forces in opposing the U.S. imperialists' air and naval war of destruction is: positively to annihilate the enemy, protect the targets the enemy wants to hit, and preserve and improve our forces. Only by succeeding in destroying the enemy can we protect our targets from him and preserve and improve our forces. Conversely, only by succeeding in protecting these targets and preserving and improving our forces can we create favorable conditions to annihilate the enemy. Judging concrete situations, sometimes we regard annihilating the enemy as the main task and sometimes protecting targets from him. Yet normally the principle of positively destroying the enemy is the most basic and most decisive content of our task.

As a result of their thorough understanding of the principle of fighting against the enemy's aircraft and warships, the northern armed forces, especially the anti-aircraft and the air force units, have created many highly effective fighting methods. Based on developing the fighting ability of each armed branch and on the coordination of many armed branches, it is necessary to pay special attention to adopting fighting methods which are most appropriate to each concrete objective of combat.

Generally speaking, the objectives of combat are the U.S. air and naval forces. However, on the battlefield in general and in each region, each direction, and each battle in particular, it is necessary to determine the concrete objective of combat, because only by doing so can we fully develop the strength of each armed branch as well as the strength of many armed branches. The basic requirement is firmly to understand the enemy's actions and our own strength and capabilities in order to determine which object must be struck, and how.

In the field of active defense, we have stepped up the people's anti-aircraft defense with the aim of restricting the losses in human lives and property caused by the U.S. Air Force and Navy. We have improved the people's anti-aircraft defense and the alert-reporting organizations and strengthened the construction and consolidation of shelters and communication trenches everywhere. We have evacuated people from the densely populated areas and adjusted the work, study, and life habits to war conditions. We have taken defense measures against the bombings and shellings of the U.S. Air Force and Navy and, at the same time, intensified the protection of security and order and taken precautionary and defense measures against the psychological warfare of the enemy, as well as against the evil plots of the reactionaries and spies.

Events during the two years of struggling against the destructive war of the U.S. imperialists prove that our defense measures have achieved great results. Although the American imperialists have caused certain damages to human lives and property of our people, basically the life of our troops and people continues to be stable, and the local economy continues to develop and agricultural production to increase; communication and transport is not interrupted, and general education, as well as other cultural and artistic activities, continue. Naturally these results have their origin in the fact that our people have satisfactorily fulfilled the task of fighting and producing at the same time. But it is obvious that the defense measures have made an important contribution to this task.

Events during the two years of struggling against the war of destruction prove that our army's and people's tactics in the struggle against enemy planes and warships are completely correct and have achieved great results. We have downed about 2,300 fighter planes of the U.S. imperialists, sunk and burned many commando boats and warships of the enemy's navy, annihilated and captured enemy pilots. We have forced the American imperialists to pay a high price for their violations of our airspace and territorial waters.

In addition to actively counterattacking the enemy's planes and warships and actively taking defense measures, we have made timely changes in our economic building and development and maintained and developed communications and transport on all lines, especially on roads leading to the frontline. This is a very important success which our people have achieved under the leadership of the party, the government, and President Ho.

Thanks to the fact that we have changed the direction of our economic building and development in good time, we have been able to pursue our socialist construction under fierce war conditions. The economy of the socialist north in wartime has satisfied the huge needs of the people's war and provided our people with sufficient strength to fight for a long time and victoriously.

On the production front, our people have strengthened revolutionary heroism, overcome all difficulties, and valiantly produced, even though the war of destruction has become increasingly fierce. Even in the areas where the enemy has attacked continuously, such as Vinh Linh, Quang Binh, and other localities, our people have stuck fast to their positions on land and sea and in factories, fighting and producing well at the same time.

Thanks to actively protecting and developing communications and transport, we have satisfactorily fulfilled the demands of the frontline, as well as those of economic construction, cultural development, and the people's life. Our people have smoothed out all our difficulties and hardships and disregarded sacrifices while insuring the continuity of communications and transport with the aim of bringing a large amount of goods to the frontline and serving the front in good time and efficaciously. This is a very great exploit of important strategic significance. It has defeated the wicked and evil design of the U.S. imperialists of creating obstacles to our communications, thus hoping to stop the support of the great rear to the great frontline.

It is obvious that our people's war has defeated the war of destruction of the U.S. imperialists. In the fire of war, the socialist north has become increasingly more powerful. The all-people solidarity bloc has become increasingly firm and stable. The people's determination to oppose the Americans for national salvation has become increasingly high. Some 17 million northern compatriots are siding with 14 million southern kith and kin to struggle until final victory.

The U.S. imperialists have sustained heavy defeats in their war of destruction against the north of our country. All their strategic designs have gone bankrupt. It is obvious that the independent activities of an air force—even if it is the modern air force of the U.S. imperialists —cannot have the effect of deciding victory on the battlefield. The U.S. Air Force can cause certain damages to our people, but it surely cannot shake our people's rocklike determination to oppose the Americans for national salvation. It surely cannot save the U.S. imperialists from complete defeat in their aggressive war against the south. The north's big victories demonstrate the great power of the people's war and of the socialist system. This power has dealt and will deal heavy blows to the U.S. Air Force, smashing its so-called superiority.

Our people throughout the country have won big victories. Our people are taking advantage of these victories to rush forward and defeat the U.S. imperialist aggressors in both the north and south, win increasingly bigger victories, and win final victory.

IV

*Four Conclusions Drawn
from the Two-Year-Old
Anti-U.S., National
Salvation Resistance*

Based on the war situation of the past two years, on the heavy defeats of the U.S. imperialists, and on the big victories of our people, we can draw the following four conclusions:

1. Our people won big victories during a very im-

portant phase of the limited-war strategy of the U.S. imperialists. The capability of inflicting complete military defeat upon more than 1 million U.S., puppet, and satellite troops is becoming a reality.

It can be said that the last two years constitute a very important phase in the limited-war strategy of the American imperialists. They have exerted very great war efforts. During the last two years, they have increased their troops massively, boosting quickly the total of U.S. expeditionary troops in South Viet-Nam from 50,000 to about 500,000 men and the total of U.S., puppet, and satellite troops to over 1 million men. They have concentrated their troops to launch two strategic counter-offensives in South Viet-Nam and, at the same time, undertaken very serious escalation steps in their war of destruction against North Viet-Nam. They have poured an enormous quantity of modern war means into the battlefield and resorted to very cruel war measures, hoping to achieve a decisive victory and bring the war to a turning point.

But they have sustained heavy defeats. They have not only been unable to achieve a turning point toward victory but have been forced to take a step backward toward defeat. All their strategic objectives—from searching for and destroying the enemy's regulars, pacifying the countryside, consolidating the puppet army, and stabilizing the Saigon puppet government to encircling and isolating the southern revolution—have gone bankrupt ignominiously. The strategic efficiency of U.S. troops has been obviously reduced. As for the puppet troops, they seem to be losing in combat activity.

During the past two years, our people have passed

through many fierce challenges and achieved many big victories, victories having a strategic meaning in both military and political fields. On the southern battlefield —a decisive battlefield—the army and people of the heroic south, under the glorious NLF banner, have developed the great people's war to an unprecedentedly high level by stepping up both the military and political struggles and by continually attacking the enemy. The compatriots and liberation forces in the south have annihilated an important part of the U.S., puppet, and satellite military forces, developed their own military and political forces very quickly, caused the balance of forces to tilt in our favor day by day, further developed their initiative on the battlefield, consolidated the liberated areas, further enlarged the front for uniting all the people for the anti-U.S., national salvation struggle, isolated the U.S. aggressors and the country-selling traitors, and continuously heightened the determination of all the people to fight and win.

On the northern battlefield, our army and people under the leadership of the party, headed by respected and beloved President Ho, have successively defeated all the war escalation steps of the U.S. imperialists and inflicted heavy losses upon them, thus causing them to become more embarrassed and stalemated in their aggressive war on Viet-Nam. The increasingly strong and powerful socialist north has been greatly developing its role of the great rear toward the great frontline.

The victories that our people throughout the country have won during the past two years are comprehensive victories in the military and political fields. In the recent past, the U.S. imperialists have concentrated their troops on carrying out their war policy in order to invade our country. That is why our people have been forced to concentrate our troops and activities on the task of defeating the U.S. bandits on the battlefield. Our people are defeating an army of over 1 million U.S., puppet, and satellite troops.

This is a military victory of great significance, a heavy blow at the aggressive will of the American war maniacs who are using the policy of force to subdue our people and conquer the south of our country. This great victory of our army and people is eloquent proof demonstrating the great power of the people's war of our country; it is a firm argument upon which we can base our conclusion that we are fully able completely to defeat over 1 million U.S., puppet, and satellite troops in the military field. This ability is becoming a reality.

2. Our people's victory is first of all the victory of the people's warfare strategy and tactics and is the anti-U.S., national salvation victory.

The victory of an armed struggle depends on many factors: the nature of the war, the comparison of forces in the two camps, the strength and quality of the armed forces, the fighting spirit of the armed forces and people, economic and military potentials, strategic and tactical leadership, international assistance, and so forth.

With respect to our country, which is small and not populous and which has to oppose an imperialist ringleader who has carried out a great military build-up with powerful weapons, not only must we have great determination to fight and win, but we must also know how to fight and to win, that is, we must have a good fighting method to be able to defeat the enemy.

The people's warfare strategy and tactics, an important part of our anti-U.S., national salvation struggle, not only have developed the determination to fight and win and the latent potential of our people, but have also developed to the utmost the intelligence and stratagems of our people to defeat the enemy. Our people's warfare strategy and tactics have succeeded in concentrating their creativeness under the leadership of a correct political and military policy. Moreover, with the experiences of our ancestors in the struggle against foreign invaders in olden days and those of revolutionary wars in other countries, they brought about glorious victories in our people's resistance against the French colonialists.

Today, our people's-war strategy and tactics have further evolved in an inspiring and creative manner, have defeated the Americans and puppets in their special-war strategy, and are defeating them in their limited-war strategy. During the past years, our people's-war strategy and tactics have directly tested their strength with that of the strategy and tactics of the U.S. imperialists, the archimperialists, in whom the essence of bourgeois military doctrine is concentrated. Through challenges, our people's-war strategy and tactics have demonstrated their superiority and invincible strength, whereas the enemy's strategy and tactics have proved to be ineffective, old, weak, and decadent along with the decadence and decline of imperialism.

Our people's-war strategy and tactics have radically upset the bourgeois military doctrine's viewpoint on the balance of power between two sides and have driven the imperialists' doctrine on relying upon weapons to complete bankruptcy. This strategy and tactics have driven the enemy into a situation in which his forces remain insufficient, even though they are numerous. He is slow, even though he possesses high mobility. He fails to acquire strength on the offensive as well as on the defensive, even though he has large numbers of aircraft, artillery pieces, and mechanized vehicles.

Besides, he has exhibited many weaknesses and pitfalls. Although the war has not yet come to an end, it is fitting to say that our people's-war strategy and tactics have defeated the Americans' limited-war strategy and tactics. The achievements and invincible strength of our people's-war strategy and tactics are paving the way for greater successes in the days ahead. In a war, once one has fallen into a strategic and tactical stalemate, he can by no means ward off his final defeat even if he possesses plenty of troops, weapons, and money. This is the situation in which the U.S. imperialists find themselves.

The great successes achieved by our people have proved that our anti-U.S., national salvation doctrine is completely correct, reflecting not only the ironlike determination of our armed forces and people, but also the fact that in adopting this line we have ourselves firmly grasped the military science of Marxism-Leninism and the art of war leadership, made a scientific analysis of our own strong points and weaknesses and those of the enemy and of the balance of power between both sides, correctly evaluated the enemy's scheme, thereby setting forth a proper direction with a view to achieving success for our people's resistance.

This line has mobilized and organized all our people and has developed the strength of our entire country to defeat the U.S. aggressors. It has been deeply imbued with the spirit of independence and of relying mainly on our own strength, while attaching great importance to the assistance of the fraternal socialist countries and the progressive people all over the world, including the progressive American people. This line has not only held aloft the patriotic banner of our people's struggle for independence and freedom but has also highly demonstrated our people's proletarian international spirit, because our people's anti-U.S., national salvation struggle is an important contribution to the common struggle for peace, national independence, democracy, and socialism waged by progressive people throughout the world.

It is for this reason that the prestige of our resistance has been increasingly enhanced and the support of the world's peoples for our people has become more and more vigorous. No national liberation struggle in history has ever obtained as much vigorous and comprehensive sympathy and support from the world's peoples as does our people's anti-U.S., national salvation resistance today. The American imperialists have sought by every means to weaken our resistance forces. Yet, they have failed. They have been disastrously isolated in the world. The success of the anti-U.S., national salvation line is also the glorious success of our party's true Marxist-Leninist line and the spirit of independence, self-reliance, and international solidarity.

3. The longer the fight, the more mature our forces, and the weaker the enemy forces. Through our anti-U.S., national resistance, all forces of our people have gone through ordeals and become increasingly mature. On the vast frontline, through two years of direct confrontation with American expeditionary troops, not only

have the southern army and people scored great achievements, but they have also gained many rich fighting experiences. The LAF has become increasingly mature, its fighting effect and strategic efficiency have been more and more increased, and its offensive impetus has become stronger and stronger.

The NLF of South Viet-Nam has been increasingly consolidated and enlarged and has continuously strengthened the people's political forces. The liberated areas have been enlarged and firmly consolidated. The political struggle movement has been widely developed. The people in the southern cities are rising up to struggle more and more fiercely against the U.S. aggressors and the country-selling Vietnamese traitors.

In the north, as the people's armed forces have been developed in quantity, as their quality has been increased, and as they have also learned from the southern LAF's fighting experiences, their fighting strength has been comprehensively increased.

The U.S. imperialists have attacked the north in a very fierce manner, but our people have never been shaken, and their determination to fight has constantly been heightened. Our army and people have ever more valiantly engaged in production and combat, are determined to insure good communications and transportation, and have devoted themselves to supporting the frontline. Never before was the friendly and brotherly northern-southern love expressed so ardently and deeply as it is now by the 17 million northern compatriots in their production and combat efforts and in support of the frontline. The northern army and people fear no sacrifices and hardships and are devoting efforts day and night to fulfilling their task toward the vast frontline with the spirit of "all for the frontline and all for victory."

As for the enemy, although his economic and military potential is great, it is, however, obvious that the more he intensifies the war of aggression in Viet-Nam, the more weakened he becomes, and the more difficulties he encounters. Although great, the U.S. military forces have been scattered in many parts of the world. The U.S. imperialists must cope with the national liberation movement, with the socialist bloc, with the American people, and with other imperialist countries.

The U.S. imperialists cannot mobilize all their forces for the war of aggression in Viet-Nam. The present mobilization level has far exceeded initial U.S. forecasts and is at sharp variance with U.S. global strategy. At present, the United States does not have enough troops to meet Westmoreland's requirements. In the days ahead, even if the U.S. imperialists send more forces to the south, they will remain unable to stop the decline of the U.S. expeditionary and puppet troops.

The American troops' fighting spirit has declined, and the leadership of the U.S. officers is very poor. Westmoreland remains unable to find any means to help the U.S. imperialists extricate themselves from their deadlocked situation, and to discover any way to help increase the U.S. troops' efficiency and to recover the puppet troops' strength, which has become more and more exhausted.

The enemy's weakness stems from his contradictions and his basic weak points, but is also attributable to a decisive factor: The invincible strength and the great achievements of our people.

Our maturity stems from the radiantly just cause of the anti-U.S., national salvation resistance, the all-people great unity bloc and the determination to fight and win, the correct anti-U.S., national salvation lines, and the strategies and tactics of the undefeatable people's war, the tenacious, indomitable tradition, the potential strength and the fighting experiences of our people in countering foreign aggression, the absolute superiority of the vast rear—the socialist north—and the strong and wide sympathy and support of brotherly socialist countries and progressive people of the world. Facts in the past years have proved that the more we fight the stronger we become, and the more the enemy fights the weaker he becomes. This is the law of the protracted, hard, but certainly victorious resistance of our people.

4. The past great achievements are a firm base on which our people can move forward to win final victory. The enemy's heavy setbacks will certainly lead him to complete defeat. At the outset, everything is difficult to do. In the past two years, the anti-U.S., national salvation resistance of our people has gone through intense ordeals and, initially, has defeated the U.S. imperialists' limited-war strategy. As we have succeeded in overcoming all difficulties at the beginning, we will certainly succeed in overcoming all the forthcoming difficulties and hardships in a more advantageous manner. The recent great achievements are a firm base from which our people can move forward to win final victory.

We do not subjectively evaluate our successes. President Ho has said: "The nearer victory is, the more hardships there will be." The U.S. imperialists are still very stubborn and cunning. Yet, no matter how frantically they may writhe, they will certainly not be able to change the situation to avoid final defeat. They can by no means turn the cause of defeat into the cause of victory but will merely deepen the causes leading them toward defeat. Taylor himself, who initiated the flexible-reaction strategy and who once directly led the U.S. war of aggression in Viet-Nam, had to admit in his latest work entitled *Responsibility and Response* that the Americans committed an error in choosing the time, place, and objective in this war. Taylor complained that the Americans have sent troops to South Viet-Nam in an instinctive rather than a calculated manner and that the Americans committed themselves too late yet too deeply to a war that is very costly in terms of human and material resources. He says that the puppet Saigon army and administration are too weak, are on the decline, and so forth.

The U.S. imperialists will certainly meet with complete defeat in their war of aggression in Viet-Nam, because they have encountered a people who not only have a determination to fight and win, but who also know how to fight and defeat all aggressive enemies. The territory of Viet-Nam is not vast and its population is not large. Yet, the Vietnamese people possess traditions of indomitableness and a very high spirit of self-reliance and have defeated all aggressive enemies. In the past few decades, our Vietnamese people, relying mainly on their own strength, defeated the Japanese fascists and the French colonialist aggressors and the U.S. interventionists. Today our people have defeated the Americans' special-war strategy and are defeating more than 1 million U.S., puppet, and satellite troops in their limited-war strategy.

This eloquent fact proves that in the present age, even though a people is small, it can have a determination to unite and fight for independence and freedom in accordance with correct and creative political and military lines, know how to rely mainly on its own strength, how to develop the favorable conditions of the time, and how to launch a people's war in conformity with the characteristics and situation in its own country. Having effective fighting methods, the people are fully capable of defeating and will certainly defeat all aggressive enemies, including the U.S. imperialists.

Can a small country, which relies mainly upon its own strength, defeat the limited war of aggression of the American imperialists, the archimperialists who possess great military and economic potentials? This is the burning question of our time. The Vietnamese people are replying to this question with their great victories. These victories are the Vietnamese people's great contribution to the world's peoples. History has entrusted this glorious mission to our people, who are resolved to devote all their minds and abilities to totally defeating the U.S. aggressors and thereby to fulfilling this historic task.

V

The U.S. Imperialists' Forthcoming Plots and Our Task

The U.S. imperialists are confronted with a tragic war situation. On the military front, their strategy has proven ineffective and failing. Following the failure of the two large-scale strategic counteroffensives, the American imperialists are now at a crossroad. Must the war be limited or expanded? If the war is to be expanded, to what degree must it be enlarged? Must efforts be concentrated mainly on stepping up the war of aggression in the south or seeking a turning point by attacking the north? Since the quick victory strategy met with failure and since it is necessary to fight a protracted war, how long will it drag on? What is to be done to increase the U.S. troops' fighting efficiency, which is very poor, to strengthen the puppet troops, who have increasingly declined, and to escape an inert, scattered, and defensive position, and to carry out an offensive strategy?

All these strategic problems are puzzling and very urgent for the U.S. imperialists. From Johnson and Mc-Namara to Westmoreland, they all have clearly realized their bogged-down and deadlocked situation in Viet-Nam but have not yet found any new solution. They have, at last, resorted to the troop-reinforcement measure. However, they are encountering big difficulties with this problem. If small reinforcements are sent in, it will be impossible to remedy the situation of the U.S. troops who are endangered on the battlefields. If large reinforcements are sent, this will greatly influence the American people's political and economic life and the U.S. strategy in the world and will not succeed in saving the U.S. imperialists from complete failure.

On the political front, the pacification mission has met with greater and greater failure and has made no progress. The puppet troops have been increasingly weakened and have lost more and more of their strategic efficiency. Following the deceitful election, the puppet administration remains unable to escape its conflicting, confused, and lost situation. The conflicts among the lackeys of the Americans, among the puppet generals, and between the military faction and the civilian cliques have become ever more acute.

The U.S. imperialists resorted to the deceitful election farce with the aim of applying a new layer of paint on the Thieu-Ky clique. However, through this farce, the Thieu-Ky clique has been exposed ever more clearly as country-selling Vietnamese traitors and lackeys of the Americans. U.S. public opinion also acknowledged that Thieu and Ky are shameless and inefficient. The puppet Saigon administration has become more and more isolated and imperiled in the face of the widespread and vigorous development of the struggle of the heroic southern army and people.

In the international arena, the American imperialists are also confronted with new difficulties. Since they have been tied firmly to the war of aggression in Viet-Nam and have suffered one failure after another, the U.S. imperialists have increasingly revealed their weaknesses and flaws. Revolutionary people the world over have more clearly realized that the U.S. imperialists are wealthy but not strong and that their economic and military potentials, although great, are nonetheless limited. The American imperialists are being defeated by a small but heroic people. The more they prolong the war of aggression in Viet-Nam, the more the U.S. imperialists are isolated politically in the world.

In the present conflict in the Middle East and Near East, the U.S. imperialists have to cope with a new front. The temporary military victories of the Israeli mercenaries, the lackeys of the Americans, did not put an end to the boiling national liberation movement of the Arab countries in this area but were an event that marked a new step of this movement. The people in the Arab countries are firmly pursuing their struggle and will certainly pursue it to liberate themselves. The temporary victories of the U.S. imperialists and the Israeli mercenaries have become their own strategic mistakes and are causing them increasingly greater difficulties in all fields.

In Latin America, which the U.S. imperialists have always considered their own backyard, the revolutionary movement has been developed vigorously, and the Latin American people have stood up against the American imperialists' interventionist and aggressive policy and the reactionary governments, the lackeys of the Americans, in this part of the world.

In the United States itself, the Johnson government is confronted with the contradictions between the U.S. ruling clique and the U.S. people's increasingly stronger protest. The American Negroes' boiling and widespread struggle is a fierce offensive blow dealt at the Johnson clique's domestic and foreign policies. Never before has President Johnson been so deadlocked as he is now. On August 14, 1967, *U.S. News & World Report* admitted that war, racial conflict, the growing budget deficit, and troubles with the Congress, with the allies, and with the dollar are bad news, putting pressure on the government from all directions. Suddenly, the situation at the White House has become like that of a building whose roof is about to cave in.

Although they are encountering difficulties and stalemate in Viet-Nam, in the world, and even in the United

States because of their stubborn, warlike, and aggressive nature and because they possess economic and military potentials, the U.S. imperialists still continue to adopt a policy of military strength in prosecuting their war of aggression in our country. What are the U.S. imperialists' plans?

1. They will continue to step up the limited war on a large scale by increasing the number of American troops in the south and staging fierce raids against the north. After making extensive calculations and weighing the pros and cons, Johnson has decided to increase the number of U.S. troops in the south by another 50,000 men, thus bringing the total of U.S. forces in South Viet-Nam, to over 500,000 by July, 1968.

Yet, the U.S. imperialists are in a difficult and stalemated situation in Viet-Nam not because they lack troops, but because their war of aggression is unjust, because they have committed many errors in exerting leadership over the war, and because they have been in a strategic stalemate and tactical crisis. For this reason, even if they increase their troops by another 50,000, 100,000, or more, they cannot extricate themselves from their comprehensive stalemate in the southern part of our country. They cannot overcome their scattered and defensive battle position, cannot achieve any turning point favorable to them, and they cannot, by any means, cope with the increasingly vigorous and resolute offensive thrust of the heroic southern armed forces and people.

It can be asserted that even if they increase the number of American troops in the south by another 100,000, 200,000, or more, the U.S. imperialists will certainly sustain more serious defeats in the southern part of our country.

Recently, on his ninth trip to Saigon, McNamara urged Westmoreland to improve the efficiency of the present number of American troops in the south, in order to raise the present combat ratio of one out of eight U.S. servicemen. Yet, how can Westmoreland do so at a time when U.S. and puppet troops are scattered in many areas and performing many tasks? This situation is irremediable. The organization of the U.S. troops depends heavily upon war equipment and technology and, as a result, it is very cumbersome and requires enormous logistical support. If technical armaments and logistical supplies were reduced, the U.S. troops would not be able to perform their combat mission, because they would be deprived of what they regard as their strength. After all is said and done, the ratio of U.S. expeditionary troops actually engaged in combat will continue to be low. This is a bitter fact, a weakness, and a major difficulty for the U.S. imperialist aggressors.

The American imperialists are planning to build a barrier along the temporary military demarcation line. Yet, no well-fortified barrier can avoid collapsing in the face of our people's strength. As a result of the construction of this barrier, U.S. troops would become more scattered and would be trapped in an inert and defensive situation.

The U.S. imperialists hold that to settle the war rapidly, it is necessary for their air and naval forces to intensify their raids against the north. They are stepping up their strikes at our lines of communication on land and on waterways, industrial establishments, cities and towns, populated areas, and so forth. Yet, McNamara himself recently admitted that with the bombing of new targets in the north, no matter what results it may bring, the United States cannot win or shorten the war and that the problem is that the war must be settled on the ground in South Viet-Nam.

At present, in their stalemated situation, the American imperialists will writhe even more frantically. They may stage fierce strikes against our cities, villages, and populated areas, further intensify their strikes against our lines of communications, step up their bombing and strafing of our dams and dikes, and strengthen their blockade of our coastal areas. Nevertheless, they definitely cannot shake our people's determination to defeat completely the U.S. aggressors in order to protect the north, liberate the south, and proceed toward reunifying the fatherland.

Our people are not afraid of undertaking sacrifices and hardships and are not afraid of any threat of the Americans. With their intense patriotism, their intelligence and creativeness, and their tremendous organizational ability, our people are resolved to make the north more and more powerful economically and in the field of national defense to insure that production achieves further progress amid the flames of war, to insure uninterrupted communications and transport under all circumstances, and that all our people's needs, especially the requirements of the frontline, are met.

Using a large expeditionary corps to wage aggression in the southern part of our country is one of the most serious strategic errors in the history of U.S. imperialism. In this error, the use of air and naval forces to extend the war to the northern part of our country is also one of the most serious mistakes and one of the most stupid measures adopted by the U.S. imperialists. Regardless of this fact, the U.S. general and field-grade officers at the Pentagon have claimed that only by escalating the war against the north can the initiative be regained and the situation reversed.

It is obvious that, faced with continuous defeats, the stupid U.S. imperialists have become more stupid. The more they increase the number of their troops and the further they escalate the war of destruction against the north, the more isolated they become politically and the more ignominious defeats they will sustain not only in the north but also in the south, and mainly in the south.

2. The U.S. imperialists may adventurously expand their limited war all over our country. We have adequately prepared ourselves to cope with this possibility. If the American imperialists expand the limited war to the north, it is certain that they will meet with complete defeat rapidly. Although they have more than 1 million troops at their disposal, the U.S. imperialists have been defeated in the south. If they expand the war to the north with infantry troops, how many more troops would be needed? Attacking the north means opening another large battlefield. The American imperialists' forces would become more scattered and would be annihilated more easily.

We have adequately prepared ourselves and are ready to deal destructive blows at the U.S. imperialists if they adventurously send infantry troops to the north. If they expand the war to the north, the war would become more complex, because by attacking the north they would be attacking the mainland of a member country of the socialist camp. In this enlarged war, the U.S. imperialists would meet with incalculably serious consequences. The war would not develop according to the American imperialists' subjective expectations. It would also depend on the policy and actions of their adversary. Our people are prepared to annihilate the aggressors.

The U.S. imperialists may extend the war to the Kingdom of Laos and intensify their provocations against the Kingdom of Cambodia. The U.S. imperialists have been put on the defensive and defeated in their aggression in South Viet-Nam. If they expand the war all over the Indochinese peninsula, they will certainly encounter greater difficulties and sustain more serious defeats. The Vietnamese, Laotian, and Cambodian peoples, united in life as well as in death, will fight side by side against the common enemy, the U.S. imperialist aggressors, to gain complete victory for the three brotherly peoples on their beloved Indochina peninsula. All the activities of the American imperialists clearly prove that they are very obdurate. Despite their bitter defeats, they still persist in continuing their aggression against the southern part of our country. They are striving to step up their criminal war of aggression.

Faced with this situation, the anti-U.S., national salvation resistance of our people sets forth new great and urgent tasks and requirements. With the great victories they have scored, our people in both zones will closely unite, overcome all difficulties and hardships, strongly develop their offensive position, resolutely smash all war attempts of the U.S. imperialists, rush ahead and completely defeat over 1 million American, rebel, and satellite troops, fulfill the glorious historical mission, and lead the anti-U.S., national salvation enterprise to final victory.

In South Viet-Nam, the great frontline of the father-land, our compatriots and the heroic LAF have not ceased enhancing their indomitable spirit, bravery, and intelligence, overcoming all hard tests, and writing the most glorious pages in history of the heroic Vietnamese people. The South Vietnamese people have raised high their victorious banner and have shown themselves worthy of the unconquerable traditions of Nguyen Dinh Chieu, Truong Dinh, Thu Khoa Huan, of the Nam Ky uprising traditions, worthy of the title of the brass fortress of the fatherland, and of the confidence of the whole nation and of beloved President Ho.

The South Vietnamese people are heroic. The whole nation is directing its eyes toward our compatriots and the combatants of South Viet-Nam and is closely unit-ing with South Viet-Nam in the unshakable belief that the South Vietnamese people will certainly be victorious and the Vietnamese people will certainly be victorious. Under the NLF leadership, the armed forces and people of South Viet-Nam are striving to build up their vic-tories, harassing the enemy, developing their initiatives, and stepping up the people's warfare on the various battlefields.

Following the victorious 1966–67 winter-spring cam-paign, the armed forces and people of South Viet-Nam are rushing forward and attacking the enemy on both fields, military and political, in the mountain and delta regions as well as in urban centers. From Tro Thien, the Fifth Zone, and the Tay Nguyen high plateau, to eastern, central, and western Nam Bo, the guerrilla and large-size forces are strongly developing their effectiveness, inflicting heavy losses on the enemy, and driving the enemy further into a stalemate.

On the South Viet-Nam battlefield, the LAF is clearly showing its ability in destroying U.S. battalions and puppet battle groups. In the days ahead, the LAF will certainly hit hard and score great victories. It will repeatedly harass the enemy and destroy many large U.S. and rebel units and achieve more resounding victories. On the South Viet-Nam battlefield, the guerrilla activities have been further developed. In the days ahead, these activities will clearly show their efficacy in annihilating the enemy everywhere, scattering him in order to fight him, and together with large-size battles, scoring many greater victories.

Along with military activities in South Viet-Nam, the political struggles are directly affecting the enemy, destroying the fighting will of American troops, and dismantling the rebel administration and armed forces. In the days ahead, the political struggle of the South Vietnamese people, especially those in the urban centers, will certainly score many glorious victories. In developing the victorious 1966–67 campaign, along with the repeated and over-all attacks against the enemy, the armed forces and people of South Viet-Nam are striving to strengthen and develop the liberated areas and to mobilize more manpower and wealth to step up further the resistance and lead it to final victory.

In mid-August, in an enthusiastic atmosphere of the resounding victories throughout the South Viet-Nam battlefields, the NLF held an extraordinary session to approve the front's political program, aimed at developing further the past great victories of the South Viet-Nam revolution, meeting the present requirements of the situation and the revolution, and paving the way for greater victories in the anti-U.S., national salvation struggle of the heroic South Vietnamese people.

The political program set forth the national salvation objectives and tasks of our southern people: to unite all the people, resolutely to defeat the U.S. imperialists' war of aggression, to overthrow the puppet administration, to form a broad national and democratic coalition administration, to build an independent, democratic, peaceful, neutral, and prosperous South Viet-Nam, and to proceed toward peaceful reunification of the fatherland. The front's political program is the heroic southern people's great national unity banner, a banner of determination to fight and win, and a banner of determination to defeat completely the U.S. aggressors. It is a bugle call which urges the 14 million southern people to take advantage of their victories to surge forward to defeat more than 1 million U.S., puppet, and satellite troops and win great and heroic victories.

In the light of the political program recently proclaimed by the front, the heroic southern people will certainly develop vigorously all their potential capabilities and their offensive thrust, step up their armed and political struggle, develop the great people's war to a new degree, and completely defeat the U.S. aggressors and their lackeys.

In the north, under the leadership of the party Central Committee and government headed by respected and beloved President Ho, our armed forces and people are simultaneously engaged, wholeheartedly and to the best of their ability, in production and combat and in resolutely fulfilling the large rear base's obligation toward the large frontline. For more than two years, our northern armed forces and people have overcome all difficulties, fought courageously, and scored many great achievements in production and combat and in serving the frontline. Our fight will be more violent in the days ahead. Therefore, the tasks of our armed forces and people will be heavier and require us to make outstanding efforts to achieve greater successes in all fields.

The present glorious and heavy tasks of the north, which have been set forth by our party, government, and President Ho, are: "simultaneously to perform production and combat, to pool human and material resources, to contribute toward defeating the enemy's war of destruction against the north, determinedly to step up production under all war circumstances, to support the southern revolution wholeheartedly and to the best of our ability, and, at the same time, to take precautionary measures against the U.S. imperialists' schemes to expand the limited war all over our country." We must thoroughly and deeply grasp these tasks and strive resolutely to carry them out by every means. On the struggle front, we must step up the people's war, resolutely defeat the U.S. imperialists' war of destruction against the northern part of our country, and hold aloft the banner of determination to defeat the U.S. aggressors through valiant and skillful acts.

Our armed forces and people must appropriately punish all new war escalation steps taken by the U.S. imperialists. We must vigorously develop the moral, material, political, and military strength of the socialist north and, at the same time, effectively use the assistance of the socialist countries in order to defeat the U.S. aggressors. We must regularly heighten our vigilance and firmly grasp the continuous, protracted, and resolute character of our task of fighting against the U.S. imperialists' war of destruction. We have never nourished any illusions about the American imperialists' good will for peace. Only by dealing vigorous and continuous blows to their air, naval, and artillery forces, inflicting heavy losses on them, and reducing their forces and aggressive determination can we check their criminal hands. Dealing vigorous and continuous blows to the U.S. imperialists' air, naval, and artillery forces constitutes the most realistic and most effective act aimed at insuring coordination with the heroic southern armed forces and people and, at the same time, is a great encouragement for the armed forces and people all over our country.

We must strive to develop the fighting capacity of our armed forces and the various branches of the people's army and make our fire nets against U.S. aircraft, warships, and artillery units increasingly effective in order to destroy as many American aircraft, warships, and artillery units as possible and to protect the socialist north more satisfactorily.

We must invent more methods of fighting the U.S. Air Force. For more than two years, as of September 14, 1967, the U.S. imperialists have had about 2,300 aircraft shot down over the north. This indicates the tragic bankruptcy of the U.S. Air Force's tactics and proves that we have had creative and appropriate tactics developed by each of our forces and branches.

Now faced with the U.S. imperialists' new plots and acts of sabotage, it is all the more necessary for us to devise braver and more resourceful tactics in order constantly to take the enemy by surprise and to cause him to sustain heavy defeats. We must also pay great attention to improving and developing methods of fighting the U.S. naval force and artillery units. With a steadfast, militant determination, heroism, courage, and intelligence, we must do our best to develop the superiority of our existing weapons and be determined to invent highly effective tactics in order to punish the American naval force and artillery units appropriately.

Along with positively fighting the enemy, we must better perform our air defense tasks. It is necessary to continue consolidating our people's air defense system, to consolidate and develop our alert network against the enemy's aircraft and warship attacks, and to consolidate and build more shelters and communication trenches, especially in densely populated places like factories, hospitals, schools, and so forth. It is necessary to promptly commend and reward individuals, units, and localities for their achievements in people's air defense. At the same time, appropriate disciplinary measures must be taken against individuals, units, and localities for neglecting air defense tasks, a negligence which may cause avoidable damage and losses.

On the communications and transportation front, our soldiers and people have made great efforts, have fought valiantly and heroically, and have scored outstanding achievements. In the days to come, we must make greater efforts in order to achieve more glorious victories on this front. No matter how fierce and ruthless enemy attacks may be, we must be resolved to insure smooth communication operations to meet the demands of the frontline and of combat and production and to insure the people's livelihood.

While continuing their resistance against the U.S. imperialists' war of destruction, the northern armed forces and people have not stopped preparing to fight and defeat the enemy if he should venture to expand the local war to North Viet-Nam. We must continue making more careful and urgent ideological and organizational preparations for vanquishing the U.S. ground force, as well as any of the enemy's armed services, on whatever scale. We must closely combine our fighting against the war of destruction with those preparations in order to defeat the enemy under all other war circumstances.

With regard to production, we must positively implement the policies and plans of the party and the state concerning the change of trends in building and developing the economy and must continue constructing the material and technical base for socialism. We must do our utmost and resolutely fulfill the state plan in order to meet the immediate demands of the anti-U.S., national salvation struggle, the demands for building socialism, and the demands of the people's everyday life.

We must step up agricultural and industrial production, attach importance to developing local industries, and endeavor to increase the economic potentials and national defense force of our people. During the past two years, under the correct leadership of the party and the government and under violent fighting conditions, North Viet-Nam's economy has demonstrated the superiority of socialism.

North Viet-Nam's socialist agriculture is settling with good results such problems as food, irrigation, intensive cultivation designed to increase production, increases in yearly crops, land clearing, and so forth. Our newborn industry has made very positive contributions to developing production, insuring the people's livelihood, and serving national defense.

On the basis of these achievements, our people can and will surely achieve socialist construction in North Viet-Nam more satisfactorily under the violent fighting conditions. The anti-U.S., national salvation struggle of our people in the entire country has entered a very urgent state. As a large rear of the entire country, North Viet-Nam is resolved to mobilize all of her manpower and wealth to carry out the slogan: "Everything for the frontline, everything for victory."

The clear-sighted leadership of the party and the government, the unbroken solidarity of the people, the determination to fight to win, the spirit of sacrificing everything for the fatherland's independence and freedom, and the outstanding efforts of our people are the most basic guarantees for our people to have sufficient strength to fight tenaciously and protractedly and to win greater achievements and advance toward the final victory.

Our People's Armed Forces must be fully and deeply aware of the enemy's schemes and our present revolutionary and military tasks, uphold the spirit of resolutely fighting to achieve victory, and increase our fighting capacity in order to become the truly invincible armed forces of the heroic Vietnamese people. On all anti-U.S. battlefields, officers and enlisted men and units of our People's Armed Forces have performed thousands of heroic acts. On all anti-U.S. battlefields, our People's Armed Forces have stood side by side with the people in raising high President Ho's banner of resolutely fighting to defeat the U.S. aggressors, and they have achieved glorious victories.

As the shock force of our people in the present anti-U.S., national salvation resistance war, our People's Armed Forces are highly enthusiastic over their achievements and feats of arms in building their ranks and fighting the enemy. We must not be subjective and conceited and must endeavor to struggle without respite to improve our fighting quality, to develop our fighting force, and to make our People's Armed Forces, which have fought well, fight better and resolve to fight to vanquish the U.S. imperialist aggressors under all circumstances of war.

The present task of our People's Armed Forces is to fight and simultaneously build themselves into an invincible steel-like force for completely defeating the U.S. aggressors. We know that to defeat the enemy, the armed forces must have a certain number of troops and at the same time be of high quality. Of these two aspects, special emphasis must be laid upon quality. To be of high quality, one company must be as strong as ten ordinary companies.

The military theory of Marxism-Leninism points out that the power of a revolutionary force must not be measured by the number of its troops alone. Quantity is necessary, but given a fixed quantity, then quality plays a decisive role. The problem of improving quality is a precious tradition and a great experience of our People's Armed Forces. From the guerrilla units of the pre-1945 general uprising period to the army units during the resistance against the French colonialist aggressors, our people's army, thanks to their high fighting quality, have used small units to defeat larger enemy units and have achieved victories everywhere.

The drives for training troops to achieve victories, for training officers and improving soldiers, and for political and military re-education have helped our People's Armed Forces fulfill, in an outstanding way, all fighting tasks during the anti-French resistance. During the past few years, the "three first" drive and the campaign for building "determination to win" units have made important contributions to making the People's Armed Forces grow quickly and win glorious victories. The burning lesson of the southern army and people who are using a force of high quality to defeat an enemy numerically superior and equipped with stronger weapons is encouraging us to struggle continually and improve the quality of our People's Armed Forces.

In the struggle against the U.S. imperialists' war of destruction, we have clearly realized the important influence of the task of improving our fighting quality. The Nguyen Viet Xuan Anti-aircraft Artillery Battalion, the 6th Missile Regiment, the 1st and 2d companies of the air force, the 7th Detachment of the navy, many artillery units, many self-defense militia units, and so forth have fought very well; they are typical examples of units having high fighting quality. The anti-French resistance of our people in the past, in its entire process as well as in the development of various battles and campaigns, has brought forth brilliant examples of the great influence of troop quality.

In the present anti-U.S., national salvation resistance, we do not have as many troops and modern weapons as the U.S. imperialists and their lackeys, yet we have defeated the enemy. This proves the great influence of troop quality. After carefully studying the strategic and fighting efficiency of the armed forces in general as well as of each category of troops, each military service, and each unit in particular, we have clearly realized the great influence of troop quality. Therefore, the problem of improving troop quality and developing fighting power is now a task of strategic significance having a decisive meaning for achieving our people's great firm decision completely to defeat the U.S. aggressors. The striving and struggling to improve troop quality and to develop the fighting power of all three categories of troops will surely increase by many times the strategic and fighting efficiency of the People's Armed Forces, achieve great progress and a big leap forward, and bring about great changes in the political and military situation of the resistance.

The problem of improving the armed forces' quality must be raised in a comprehensive way, embracing all fields: political, military, logistics, ideology, organization, and efficiency. We must implement this policy in all three categories of troops—regulars, local troops, and self-defense militiamen—in all military services and branches, and in all military organs at all echelons, with the aim of developing the power of every component of the People's Armed Forces in order to defeat the U.S. aggressors in all war circumstances.

We must endeavor to increase further the regulars' fighting capability, making all regular units fight better and actually become the iron fists which will win every battle and continually and quickly and completely annihilate the enemy everywhere in our country. We must pay more attention to increasing the fighting power of local troops in order to make these units, from the mountainous region to the coastal areas, become strong, have great fighting capacity in the localities and be able to fight well independently, as well as in cooperation with militiamen and regulars, and fulfill all tasks in an outstanding way, destroy the enemy forces, launch the guerrilla war, and protect the people.

We must pay attention to increasing the fighting power and numerical strength of the self-defense militia, thus making the self-defense militia become a strong, stable, and widespread armed force ready to fight the enemy and fight him well with all weapons, on hand or to be obtained, play the role of a shock force in production, and supply the local and regular forces with good officers and soldiers.

We must pay greater attention to increasing the quality of the armed forces' military organs and schools so that these can be of great help to military leaders and commanders, so that the schools can train and improve many officers of high quality, thus actively contributing to the fulfillment of the building and fighting task of the People's Armed Forces. We must endeavor to satisfy the following requirements:

1. To heighten the political and ideological levels

of officers and men so that they can more deeply understand the sacred anti-U.S., national salvation duty, have a vehement revolutionary spirit, a strong offensive spirit, and a high fighting will, and unite closely around the party Central Committee, the government, and President Ho, thoroughly to implement the policies and lines of the party and the instructions and orders of higher echelons, to fulfill all fighting, building, and other tasks, and have the determination totally to defeat the U.S. aggressors and win the greatest victories on the battlefield under any circumstances of war.

2. To heighten their technical and tactical levels, it is necessary to pursue the training of officers and men so that they can maintain and cleverly use their weapons and equipment and flexibly and efficiently apply the tactical principles and fighting methods of the people's war. It is necessary to place emphasis on the quality of resoluteness, courage, resourcefulness, and creativeness in combat and study. We must also pay special attention to training units so that they can launch military operations, station troops, and fight continually on all battlefields under arduous and fierce conditions.

3. To rearrange and improve organizations and equipment so as to fit them to the combat requirements, to the characteristics and duties of different units, to battlefield conditions, and to our capacity, in order to make the various units become orderly, light, and strong organizationally and have great fighting power. It is necessary to streamline the organization, arrange the forces rationally, and build for various organizations work habits and systems to be applied in military operations and combat.

4. To streamline party organizations and mass organi-

zations; to streamline party committees and branches in order to make them strong and stable in all fields, regularly to develop the party; to improve party members so that they will have a high political level and be able to mobilize the masses; to build leadership methods for various party echelons from top to bottom; continuously to heighten the leading role of the party under all circumstances; to continue streamlining the mass organizations so that these can fulfill all their tasks and missions, fully develop the intelligence and capacity of all their members, and become a great force in each unit.

5. To improve the troops' material life, heighten their technical level, and improve their stamina and endurance; strictly to enforce the systems of preserving and repairing weapons and military equipment; strictly to enforce the principle of taking weapons from the enemy to equip ourselves; satisfactorily to organize the feeding of troops, their physical training, the improvement of their endurance and stamina, and the improvement of their health, thus insuring a high percentage of fighting men; satisfactorily to organize the treatment of wounded and sick troops so that they will be restored and returned to their units quickly.

6. To develop and increase the efficiency of cadres at all levels. The cadres have played a very important role in building the armed forces and in improving their fighting ability. Only when the cadres are good can units become good and fulfill their fighting task and other tasks. Therefore, it is necessary to strive to develop and increase the efficiency of cadres at all levels and to pay attention to raising the troop units' leadership, command, and management level and the organizational level

in order to fulfill all concrete tasks under difficult, complicated conditions, especially under urgent, fierce fighting circumstances.

We must have a very high determination and many effective measures in order swiftly to increase the efficiency of cadres at all levels. Only on this basis can we satisfy the early maturity of the armed forces and war development. At present, the movement to raise the quality and to develop the fighting strength of the People's Armed Forces and to increase their determination to fight and defeat the U.S. aggressors is highly significant with regard to the fighting and building task of our People's Armed Forces. This movement requires all cadres and combatants to make strenuous efforts and to devote themselves to increasing the fighting strength of all units to a new, higher degree.

The leading and commanding cadres bear a very great responsibility. Cadres and party members must certainly take the lead in this important movement. All cadres, at all levels, must have a great determination to fight and completely defeat the U.S. aggressors. It is necessary to see all the enemy's setbacks, difficulties, confusion, and deadlock, and, at the same time, to see all the great successes and capabilities of our army and people, to study the enemy and ourselves in detail, and firmly to grasp the laws of the resistance and the skilled military art of the people's war. Let all cadres, at all levels, enthusiastically move forward, be more determined and valiant, and resolutely fight and defeat and know how to defeat the aggressors so as to make valuable contributions to the glorious task of our people and People's Armed Forces.

On the vast frontline, the southern LAF are simultaneously fulfilling the fighting and building tasks and have incessantly increased their fighting strength. The resounding feats of arms, the swift maturity, the outstanding progress, and the abundant achievements of the heroic southern LAF are vigorously encouraging all cadres and combatants of our People's Armed Forces. It is hoped that the heroic southern LAF will score great achievements in fulfilling their fighting task as well as in the task of increasing their fighting strength and will, together with all our people, move forward totally to defeat the U.S. aggressors.

In carrying out President Ho's sacred anti-U.S., national salvation appeal in order to defeat completely the more than 1 million U.S., puppet, and satellite troops, our People's Armed Forces must have in mind and carry out his advice: be loyal to the party and the people, fulfill all tasks, overcome all difficulties, and defeat all aggressors. All our cadres and combatants must clearly understand their tasks, strive to struggle, swiftly increase the fighting strength of the People's Armed Forces, and resolutely fulfill their glorious task as shock forces of all our people in the anti-U.S., national salvation struggle.

The victories on the battlefields are encouraging us and filling us with enthusiasm. All our people await new steps of progress and more resounding and greater feats of arms from our People's Armed Forces in the days ahead. The history of our people is the history of a victorious people. Tran Hung Dao, Le Loi, Nguyen Trai, and Quang Trung fiercely fought an enemy of greater strength and were gloriously victorious.

Since the party and President Ho assumed leadership, our people have brought to success the August Revolution and the resistance and successively defeated the Japanese fascists, the French imperialists, and the U.S. interventionists. In the past ten years, our people have successively defeated all the aggressive schemes of the U.S. imperialists, their neocolonialist aggressive policy and their traditional tricks, their special war fought with more than 500,000 puppet troops, and have defeated and are defeating their limited-war strategy fought with more than 1 million U.S., puppet, and satellite troops in the south and have, at the same time, defeated and are defeating their air and naval war of destruction in the north.

It is obvious that our Vietnamese people have sufficient determination and capabilities and will certainly and completely defeat the U.S. invaders' war of aggression. In the fierce fight against the U.S. aggressors, the most cruel and barbarous imperialist ringleaders of the present war, our Vietnamese people will certainly achieve complete victory, because our great national salvation resistance has been glowing with just cause, has enjoyed correct political and military doctrine and the united strength of our people who rose up to struggle, has possessed a firm determination and skilled fighting methods, and has enjoyed great assistance from the brotherly socialist countries and strong sympathy and encouragement from progressive people of the world, including the American people.

The anti-U.S., national salvation resistance of our people is the continuation and development of the August revolutionary struggle and the anti-French resistance of the past. This resistance must entail a great many sacrifices and hardships but will certainly score glorious successes. This is the great struggle, which has never been seen before in the history of our people to build and protect the country. This struggle is also of great international significance, because it contributes to protecting the socialist bloc and advancing the movement to liberate the peoples and to protect the peace of the world. It is a great contribution of our Vietnamese people to the common revolutionary struggle of the people of the world to oppose imperialism, headed by the U.S. imperialists, and to achieve peace, national independence, democracy, and socialism.

Under President Ho's banner calling for "determination to defeat the U.S. aggressors," let all our army and people take advantage of victories to move forward. The Vietnamese people are determined to defeat completely more than 1 million U.S., puppet, and satellite troops. The U.S. imperialists' neocolonialist war of aggression will certainly be defeated. The people's war of the heroic Vietnamese people will certainly win complete victory.